Never Got The Memo...

By: Gail J. Kueker

Never Got The Memo...
By: Gail J. Kueker
Copyright © 2018 Gail J. Kueker
All rights reserved.
ISBN: 0692913904
ISBN 13: 9780692913901

DEDICATION

Brooke and Madison Weber may you both know the splendor of following your dreams and aspirations.

To David...it is better to have LOVED and lost...then to never have LOVED at all.

Surrender is faith that the power of LOVE can accomplish anything even when you cannot foresee the outcome.

Deepak Chopra

CONTENTS

Dedication 5

Introduction 11

1 At First Site... 29

2 Self-Reflection, Redirection, and Reinvention... .. 39

3 Choosing to Write My Own Story... 51

4 Somewhere in Time... 67

5 Can I get you a Cocktail? 79

6 Following Your Heart... 91

7 California Bound... 101

8 Ruby Slippers... 113

9 Following My Inner Buddha... 125

10 Pure LOVE in a package of a…
    Soft Coated Wheaten Terrier! ... 133

11 Bonjour PARIS…Again! ... 139

12 118 W. Main Street Barrington, IL ... 147

13 New Store Location? ... 157

14 Is That You? ... 165

15 How Many Times Does One Need to
    Say Goodbye in a Lifetime? ... 179

16 The Journey Still Continues as I…
    Surrender to LOVE ... 189

17 The Audacity of Moving Forward! ... 201

Epilogue ... 223

From the Author: ... 227

You may think that this is about one person's quest for LOVE, but it's so much more than that!

The Hero is of this story is LOVE

and the

Heroine is LETTING GO...

<u>*while finding the courage to hit the RESET button!*</u>

INTRODUCTION

The title of this book has been changed numerous times throughout the years as I have written and rewritten these chapters.

My first title choice was, *Believe.Surrender.LOVE.*, but I felt that it was way too close to *Eat.Pray.LOVE.* So, I moved on to one of my personal favorites, *Surrender to LOVE*. That was until I discovered that Surrender to LOVE, was already taken.

When the title Never Got The Memo came to life, I liked it for a several of reasons. Mainly because I'm fluent in three languages English, Sarcasm, and Profanity. And I just felt that this particular title was a touch "tongue in cheek," which is prefect for me! The title satires a comfort that I have in finding my own answers in life (good or bad), while still remaining open to hear other people's opinions. But the end result will always be what I find 100% comfort in.

And finally if and when there might have ever been any kind of general memo that went out to the public at large. Stating that "we" as a member of this mass society must be concerned about what others think... especially on the topic of how "we" should choose to carry out our lives, then I definitely...*NEVER GOT THE MEMO!* #I'm the BOSS of my life and I don't wait for the extraordinary to happen to be happy...I find happiness in the ordinary!

We were never given an instruction manual at birth. Life is about "figuring it out." Even those who were raised in the healthiest of environments will still struggle with understanding "life's" adventures. Obviously, I feel that our chosen directions in life are our own, but we still need to be mindful of having mutual respect and compassion for others who don't see life the same way we do. My wish is that we can learn to support each other more, versus finding satisfaction in ridiculing each other.

This book/journal started out as a simple story of LOVE, but then it evolved into something so much more than that, it's about embracing the importance of (self) LOVE. This "dark horse" enjoys continuing to embark on personal journey's that **shatter concepts and illusions of others**. If you're bored with life's cliches and over used metaphoric manifestos, then just skip over all of this and go right to Chapter One.

...*defining LOVE!*

The essence or energy of LOVE is what keeps us all seeking, desired union of two souls. That connection of being totally accepted unconditionally by another.

What I have come to understand is that through the eyes of others-LOVE can be conditional. We don't ever like to admit this...but unfortunately it really is the truth! One of the main reasons why we struggle to accept others unconditionally...is because we're all still learning **how to embrace ourselves...unconditionally!**

Part of learning to LOVE unconditionally (mainly towards ourselves), starts with what I like to call the "secret sauce" of life. The first aspect of that secret sauce in life is a combination of discovering that you're already enough on your own. Then you move on to embracing your own sense of self-empowerment (making your own choices in life and being confident in those choices while exercising the proper use of your boundaries).

Next, it's about learning the importance of knowing your own language of LOVE (what it takes for you to feel LOVED and understood). Another major plus, is never taking yours or anyone else's dramas too seriously. And for those that seek drama to get attention, well then give it to them, but if that drama becomes the basis of your connection then maybe it's time to move on.

Life is way to short...so laugh and surround yourself with those who like to laugh too. A good sense of humor is mandatory in life. Finally, and the most difficult aspect of all-being patient while life unfolds. Understanding and embracing all of this will help you to discover and accept your strengths as well as your weaknesses. When you truly carry that type of awareness, you will be an unstoppable "force."

We as a society are riddled with so many feelings of lack to begin with, that we tend to feel a constant sense of absence in our lives. And with that absence we seek so much more from others in order to fill up those gaping holes of lack. Some may fill those "holes of lack" by creating a dependence on certain aspects in life. Such as seeking popularity-by living up to other people's ideals (social conformity), possibly selecting a certain career to gain power and prestige, or by selecting certain spouses or partners that might fit a certain "ideal." All of this to feel a sense of importance or connection to something deeper, something more intrinsic.

There are those who don't even know how to begin to gain that inner strength. So they decide to numb it away with drugs, alcohol, gambling, shopping. There are numerous ways to we use to distract or deter ourselves. Whatever the chosen form of temporarily disconnecting might be, these **dependencies lead to a slow destruction of their own soul's growth.**

You must really understand this...because that void that you may feel, can never be filled by a "chosen distraction" or another person. That void or absence, can only be magnetized or mirrored back to you by others that come into your life. Meaning, whatever you're needing to still work on you will only attract people into your life that are missing that same exact thing. This is where being aware of your strengths and weakness becomes paramount. So, you can recognize and address them and not "pretend" them away.

For example: When you first meet someone usually it's all good in "LOVEland." Especially in the beginning, because everybody is on their best behavior. As time goes on and the luster starts to wear off, that's when things that you might have found cute or endearing at the beginning, become irritating. That is why, for your relationship to keep growing, you must be able to understand, accept, and discuss what is working and what is not. Relationships are only as healthy as the people that are within them.

My objective here is not to a be a Psych 101 course. So many trail forth with so much baggage from their past because somehow they don't feel heard, understood or worse yet...many feel insignificant even though they might be in a "LOVING" relationship. So they look to others to give them, what they really should already have before they got into the relationship, and that is self-acceptance.

Our complex issues can be exactly that...complex. We must ascertain a better way to not only communicate with others, but more importantly be heard. Which can be a total lifesaver in a romantic relationships or in any kind of relationships for that matter.

Did you know that there is an actual language to LOVE?

This philosophy, is not a cure all for relationships, but it really helps you to learn how we all need to "feel" validated and LOVED in different ways. Learning these simple aspects can help you to see that we all hear and feel things differently. Don't we all want to be heard, validated and appreciated...more?

The simplest way to learn each other's LANGUAGE OF LOVE, is through the philosophy or book by Gary Chapman called, *The 5 Languages of LOVE*. In his book you will learn how you like to personally receive LOVE. Here is a very brief synopsis on the languages of LOVE.

The first aspect, is when someone takes care of you (through service), second-through the giving of gifts, third-spends "quality time" with you, fourth is-through touch, and fifth-is through words of affirmations or appreciation. The more you understand and embrace about your own unique aspects on how you **NEED** to feel LOVED, accepted, and cherished, the more it will prevent yourself from getting involved with those who neither understand nor care about how you desire to feel LOVED. For me this was a mandatory lesson to learn in relationships. Because I believe that we all want to feel safe in our connections. Otherwise then, I have a personal motto and goes like like this, **"I know what I bring to the table... so believe me when I say...that I'm not afraid to eat alone."**

The path of finding your own inner strength is so different for each individual, and no it's not based on the number of likes you get on social media or the number of friends, dates or LOVER's you have. If anything the greatest test of self-LOVE (acceptance), is just about you just being you...and finding complete comfort in your own presence.

Being 100% comfortable with your choices no matter what they are, along with having very little desire to explain yourself to anyone, should be your driving force in life. That 100% acceptance of self is projected through your smile and your openness to meet others. But, most of all it's about being able to **listen**-there is a reason why they call it "the art of listening." Proper listening is not talking over another person while they're talking. And it's especially not about hearing someone explain something, then the other person disagreeing, only to have them repeat back what was just stated almost exactly. **But, in their own words**! Seriously? Connecting with others is all about just having a general vibe of being open, being easy to be around, and most of all being sincere.

I have noticed in life that the more comfortable you are with yourself-the greater your tendency is to be more open, and compassionate towards others. And be excited for others on their endeavors in life. I have seen this so many times, people holding back from supporting and acknowledging others for any special type of accolades that they might have accomplished. Possibly due to the fact that it may divert attention away from them. Or maybe for the simple fact that it reminds them of what little they have done or maybe are even "afraid to do" in their life. Bottom line, not being supportive of friends, family, LOVE's for their accomplishments is selfish, and it only reflects badly on yourself.

Really life all comes down to "playing nice." Yep just that simple, just like we were all taught in kindergarten. Even when you don't like someone, you should always be polite.

And playing well with others really can be easy. That is until you're face-to-face with those who actually enjoy making it their personal mission in life, to be difficult. It's almost like a sport to them. They purposely create an environment of being cold, rigid, and rude, bullying you just to prove that they can exercise some form of control in their life. That control, is simply a choice to make your day difficult. That need for being "rigid" is simply about them being bullies! And I feel that one of the worst types of "bullies" are those that are nice to your face, but say belittling things behind your back. These passive-aggressive bullies also have a great tendency to be bulldozers.

I'm sure you know what I mean by being a "bulldozer"; those are the people that you meet in your personal life or in a business atmosphere that must "try" to overpower you. Driving you into their own thought patterns and desires. They will talk over you, and minimize your perspective in life. They're just overall...not nice people. People, you must learn to stay in your own lane! You need to run as fast as you can from those who do not respect you or your space! They will never change and it's not your job to educate them.

With the many personality types you will come across on your path during your lifetime, try to always stay in the OBSERVER lane, versus in the REACTION-ARY lane. It's so much safer and it saves wear and tear on your brain. Remember that everything in life is a choice...so choose wisely!

Reactionary people, are the ones that like to engage and blame others. In fact, their "major" in the school of life, is judging others for what they feel are poor choices in **their** eyes. Most of the time they like to pass on their own form of suffering to others, and not their wisdom or lessons. They usually are afraid of risks, and they never seem happy. You might see moments of happiness arise in their life. But nothing permanent...because they live in a constant state of fear and resentment.

Reaction state personalities are critical, they feel entitled, and LOVE to blame others. **They don't know how to give LOVE, because they're so used to taking LOVE and attention from others. The true language of LOVE is GIVING and then receiving.**

Being an "observer", is someone that sits back watches and takes it all in, without too much judgment. You might even say that they're "laid-back." They just never seem to let too many things rattle them, because they're just "easy to be around."

Being in the presence of someone that truly vibrates and harmonizes in LOVE and EASE, can be pure joy. But a very important caveat to understand here is that these people are not looking for total popularity or universal acceptance. Usually, because they're not trying to live by anyone else's social criteria. They have no need for social status, no desire for particular label's in clothes. Special homes to reside in, nor living up to professional expectations from others. They're easy to LOVE and like...because they actually like themselves.

When you are in the presence of someone that really enjoys who they are as a person, and what they're about...it's easy. The energy just flows. They truly wish to evolve and prosper at no one else's expense. They tend to speak clearly and directly and have little to no need to manipulate a situation. And they have even less patience for others that do enjoy manipulating people. In other words...if they do not feel that the relationship is REAL, then they have no desire to continue the connection.

They have learned to accept and give LOVE to others, without ever needing to out shine them, or overpower them. If you need to do any of those things to others, then that's just your fear showing up...telling others that you don't truly believe in yourself.

When you're with someone that's always "taking" in relationships, it's like trying to keep the same fire burning forever. It takes a lot of energy and eventually, it will have to die out. The key is knowing how to start that fire on your own-first. Then when you meet someone else that you would like to spend time with those flames will just grow bigger and more intense together with time. Knowing what you have to offer others is mandatory in life. Until you understand this and truly embrace that YOU'RE ENOUGH...nothing or no one will ever be able to fill that void that you feel.

...then what's it all about?

Basically, the subtle nuance in life is learning how to *surrender in life,* to *simply find ease to allow and* accept. Personally, I feel that this is one of the most difficult elements in life to learn and embrace completely. When trying to explain the "art" of surrendering-I define it as an ability to move through life with ease. By simply allowing and without trying to control every aspect of our life or anyone else's for that matter.

I think a lot of people would say, "Sure, yeah I do that all the time," *but do you really?* When you're truly *moving with ease* and allowing, you're TOTALLY accepting the universal direction of life without question. That means no matter what the circumstances are...trust that everything is happening and aligning for your highest good. It's actually about allowing yourself to let go of the oars of the boat completely, and seeing where the current directs you. It's not about you trying to pull the boat to where you want it to go. Now...do you want to ask yourself that again...*do you really surrender to LOVE and life daily?*

And to all of you power brokers, movers and shakers out there reading that last statement and possibly thinking, "Oh what a shame...this poor girl is so misinformed." So many of us, myself included at one time or another have felt like we constantly need to direct our lives. I believe this is true up to a certain point. Because we all have desires, passions, and needs for a reason. They're there to help direct us in life, and of course we all want those desires to be fulfilled.

What we must learn is that working hard and trying to make something occur, is really not the complete answer. That's a great start and intention, but once a desire has come into awareness, you must be **open** to how life is flowing. If you're finding **resistance** or lack of JOY in life, then chances are you're focused in the wrong direction.

So then how will you know when you're forcing life and not allowing the flow of life? That's easy...no matter how hard you try, you'll find that things just aren't working out and everything seems to be a strain. Allowing in life, is simply about never forcing or pushing things into action. Because when we try to force things into action, that is **fear grabbing the wheel.** This can be especially apparent when we're feeling that things might not be happening fast enough or worse yet, that they might not happen at all. So, we may start by overachieving out of a need to capture that elusive element of whatever you think that you need, so bad.

It can be a relationship, a certain job, or an aspiration. But when you go into that overzealous crazed action, desperately acting to hold on to something or someone, doing anything it takes, to see the results you want... that's most definitely NOT allowing and flowing with life. That's 100% RESISTANCE to life...and your ego is in-charge, demanding it go the way that you want it to go.

So, no matter what you hear about life and all its lessons and protocols, it really is as simple as LOVE and fear. No matter what metaphoric phrase that they attach to it, such as Heaven and Hell, light and dark, or good and bad. Fear is just simply resistance, and maybe it's easier for you to hear the word "resistance" instead of the word "fear", but they're the exact same thing.

Because you're either standing in the light of LOVE and allowing, embracing, and receiving the ease of life to unfold naturally. Or you're standing in the shadows of fear and resistance, and missing out on possible opportunities. Or even worse, you're demanding things go your way; but then "secretly" worried it will NOT occur at all. These are all negative reactions coming from, and protecting our "ego's."

When you find yourself not flowing with the energy of life, and you're unhappy with your job or things happening in your personal life. Maybe it's time for you to **hit the RESET button.**

Be open in life for course corrections to occur. Yes, it can be another difficult litmus test in life. But, if you don't re-align yourself and your direction, you might just find yourself being forced into an action through a divorce, getting fired, or even losing a home or business.

Those course-corrections are hard and painful and many of you may have a hard time moving on from a difficult situation because of fear. Fear that something worse will occur with that "new" choice. Causing you to stay involved in unhealthy environments and relationships.

Quite simply those fears are the *mind* "trying" to sabotage us. It can be one of the most difficult tasks in life to keep your mind quiet and to follow your heart. But once you discover that the true power of knowing, is trusting your own voice and desires that knowledge will carry you through the craziness and the chaos occuring all around us on a daily basis. The more you follow your own inner guidance, the stronger it becomes. It's like a muscle...it just gets stronger and more unstoppable with time.

Surrendering really allows you to stay present to your boundaries and what you want and don't want in your life. This philosophy of *surrendering* has nothing to do with giving up on life and letting others feel victorious. Nor, is it about allowing others to overrule and dominate your own desires in life. Many think they have the "best" answers...but only you know what the best solutions is for yourself. It's all about recognizing the sound and strength of your own words and convictions.

In times of crisis, I obviously I wanted things to go a certain way. But it wasn't until I started applying this philosophy...of completely letting go and ALLOWING that I started to see some pretty wonderful and mysterious things occur. Now, as soon as something is not moving with ease, that's my signal to let go and allow another direction. This pertains to all areas of my life, work/career, all personal relationships, even general connections with others. But don't think for a moment that I have mastered this...because I haven't. Fear sneaks into everyone's lifes from time to time. But in the midst of chaos let that be your clue to "let go," so that you can find your center again.

I truly believe that this is the nirvana that everyone is searching for in life. It's so simple and so difficult at the same time. If it were easy...everybody would have it mastered it.

You'll find blank pages throughout this book/journal to help you connect to your own personal answers while reading my story. So feel free to write, color, or even paint what comes up for you. Because it's NOT ABOUT resolving your past experiences. It's about accepting and allowing, so that you can get to your desired and intended future.

Note To Self

Note To Self

Note To Self

CHAPTER ONE

At First Site...

We're consumed with how to do LOVE right and how to make it successful, all while overcoming its problems and surviving its failures. There are many journeys of LOVE in our lives, and this is the beginning of one very unique one that occurred in my life.

It was one of those nights when I felt like I was forcing myself to go out. Cold. Rainy. The usual dreary weather during that time of year just reinforced my whole concept of not wanting to go out to begin with.

My friend and I arrived at a local nightspot in one of the northern suburbs of Chicago. We were having all of the usual drinks accompanied by all of the usual conversational topics when I happened to notice these random two guys walk through the front door. For some reason, the second guy really captured my attention right away. Not because he was strikingly handsome, it was more his "presence" that drew me to him. In fact, I had the strangest insight when I first laid eyes on him.

Back then I thought it was more like random "headspeak". But it wasn't some kind of inner dialogue. It was pure intuitive insight for which I now clearly know the difference.

This random "intuitive insight" that just popped in my head moments after first seeing him was...**"That is the man I will marry."**

Okay...where the hell did that just come from?

While trying to shake that crazy and moronic phrase off, and trying to get back into conversational mode that was occurring all around me–as I floated off somewhere. When I felt a tapping sensation on my shoulder...I turned around and was in complete shock...it was him...out of nowhere.

Now, that's strange. Because just a second ago some strange voice in my head just had us walking down the aisle together...and now here he was standing in front of me!

Needless to say, I needed to see what "this" was all about! So, instead of the usual brush off, I needed to let this boy talk.

"Excuse me, we would like to meet you both."

As the first lines fell from his mouth, it spurred me on to ask, "*Do you come with subtitles?*"

Maybe not the best reply...but effective and perhaps even a touch funny. But, like so many others...he really didn't grasp nor understand my humor. Which was incredibly obvious by his non-response. Okay...awkward!

Though he then did go on to explain that he and his friend had just come from an ESL (*English as a second language class*) being held down the street. Okay, total picture...coming together now!

Before I get too deep into this story I need you to be very aware of something, and that is that no one before, nor after him, has ever moved me the way he did that night...at first sight. I was so mysteriously drawn to him, and to have that crazy phrase go through my head was seriously strange. It was like I had already known him, without ever personally meeting him.

After that amazing first encounter, David and I dated seriously for a number of years, and we had a really good relationship. We still had all the usual ups and downs that normal couples experience, but I always had a sense of comfort and ease in his presence.

Even though we were very much a couple back then, I still had my own dreams and desires, and was determined to make my own mark in the world. But, I wanted it all, to spend time with this man that I was very much in LOVE with and my own independence to create and discover what life holds for me. Perhaps my desire for independence was a little too strong. As I look back, it could have been one of the determining factors to our demise.

Still, the day that it all went away was a moment my life stood still. At the time of our breakup I felt like I was dragging around my own special set of custom-made cement shoes. The color literally slipped

Chapter One

from my world, and, as an artist, that isn't a good thing! How could something that felt so right, go so wrong?

When I reflect back on our time together before our break up, it seemed rushed. Perhaps because of time being so fleeting. But it also seemed as though I was "trying" to find some sort of perfect balance in life. You know, that balance of having someone special in your life, plus pursuing your own direction in the world. One thing that has always been very clear to me, is that **I never wanted to be in the shadow of a man, I want to be a force of my own!** Little did I realize then how much of my own shadow, I needed to learn about and discover first.

At that time I really thought I was "trying" to follow all the typical social norms. Getting an education, building a career, then possibly getting married. Then planning that "dream home." Going off somewhere special to pick out that perfect tile, for that perfect home, that you will both spend the rest of your lives in. You know navigating all of the usual typical social expectations. What I didn't know back then, was that there was nothing typical about me.

I think that's where I was so misinformed. Back then I thought that I had to somehow acquire that LOVING relationship with someone else first. Then maybe the rest of my life would just automatically fall into place. Wrong!

Sometimes I felt, and maybe I still do, that I have more of a desire for a relationship with a career or fulfillment of a dream-than with anything else. What I know now is that I wanted to know what my own potential was in this world, more than I wanted to be a wife and mother. Even though I was never about finding the fast track to success, I was more about achieving small career goals for myself. Some may find this very limiting, but I looked at it as my own special comfort zone.

There is a famous quote from Madonna, when she was first discovered. Dick Clark interviewed her back in the day and he asked her, "What do you want to do with your career?" She answered, "I want to rule the world." In her way, and in her time, she did. I have always known what I wanted to do for a living, as long as I was working within the creative arts, I was happy. But I do think I will leave ruling the world to someone else.

Along with having that complete comfort of knowing what I wanted in my career, I also wished to live a simple and relax lifestyle. I never craved living that crazed fast-paced Chicago lifestyle. Nor was I about the traditional home in the suburbs with 2.5 kids and the dog; trying to juggle being a Mom and finding time to fit everything else in-including myself. I'm more the cozy, semi-secluded "artist's" cottage, adjacent to a lake… kind of gal.

I always knew I wanted to be a self-made woman with a simple and easy lifestyle. You would think that knowing myself so well, would allow the ease and comfort of time and circumstances to gradually fill in those empty spaces, but, I'm afraid finding that ease and acceptance would take a lot longer than I had even hoped or prayed for.

I once heard from one of the many different people that have crossed my path in my life, thus far, that I certainly came into this lifetime to learn LOVE and patience…how true they were! Learning to LOVE unconditionally and finding the patience to allow, has definitely been my NEEDED applied mantra throughout this lifetime.

Finding the balance between extremes was a longer pursuit than I ever thought possible. What I feared after "the break up" was that maybe I was too worried about my own story in life and didn't place enough attention on our relationship. Was I being too selfish or did we just want two different things from life? What caused it all going away? My journey to understanding begins.

Lesson Learned: *It's not about having desires in life that creates divides in relationships. It's when desires are all-consuming, and we forget that we have someone that needs our LOVE in return. If you need to ask yourself if there is enough time being spent together, then maybe there's not. More importantly looking at it from the standpoint of what I did WRONG, is where I went wrong.*

It's not about what I did wrong, everything happens for a reason and we were just at the end of our relationship…period!

Note To Self

Note To Self

Note To Self

Note To Self

CHAPTER TWO

Self-Reflection, Redirection, and Reinvention...

After the breakup I needed some time for a little self-pity, redirection and of course reinvention. I wanted to reinvent myself because everything that once defined me was now gone. A LOVE, and a career all simultaneously...so who the hell am I?

Back when we were together, I would have married David in a heartbeat. That's what I wanted **at that time.** Even though there were obvious signs of an appending doom towards the end, I just didn't want to recognize that it was...the end. Those signs of doom became quite evident when we started talking about taking our relationship to the next level.

We were both out at a local mall, when we discussed going to look for rings. As soon as we both entered that jewelry store, a weird energy shifted between us; it was as though David's whole demeanor had changed immediately. Maybe it was just me being too sensitive, but something just wasn't right. I turned to him and said, "H*ey...instead of us looking for rings, why don't we just go look for a suit for work?* He agreed, and we both left the jewelry store immediately.

The shift was fast and obvious. I even found relief. But relief from what? I really thought that this was something that we both wanted! Even though I knew in that exact moment it would NOT happen. I just would have never admitted it to myself back then. But, the obvious truth was that we would never be married. A couple months later we broke up for good.

...*beginning of the end!*

On that beautiful spring day in April, David called me up and said that he needed to see me. I knew the moment I heard his voice, that we were over. I really wish my intuition would take a vacation sometimes.

I met David at his place, purposely wearing an outfit that he had bought me on one of his trip's back home to Europe. Let's just say that I was trying a little too hard to make an impression. As soon as I arrived, he had asked me if I wanted to go for a drive. I'm sure he was thinking...this could get messy, so let's take it public. We ended up going to one of our usual places, we both ordered a drink. He just said it, "I just can't do it." I replied, *"Can't do what?* Of course I knew exactly what he was talking about. David shared where he was coming from and why he felt the way he did. I sat perfectly still, incapable of movement or sound. The words spilling out of him were cold, like the liquids we were drinking. That coldness was now filling my veins. He said it...he actually said it. His words can't be taken back now. Those were the very words I feared to hear the most.

There is no time now. All is one. As soon as we arrived, we left. I'm on auto-pilot. I know we're driving, because blobs of color were flying by, as I sat there staring out the passenger window, frozen. Thinking, where are we going? I didn't care. That destination did end up being the lake front (Lake Michigan). Talking and more talking. I don't really hear his words. I'm I so checked out that the only thing I really understand is that we're two souls occupying a car. I do remember the feeling the emotion of ambivalence but it didn't matter now...because Gail is gone. Her emotions are dead. This is now a murder scene, a murder of a great LOVE.

He then asked me to dinner. We had dinner-more talking. I'm thinking…are we breaking up here or what? But believe me...I was more catatonic than in the mood to be sarcastic. Perfect word, catatonic. I literally felt like someone had removed all my internal organs and I was walking around like some kind of a shell. Hollow, void of emotion, on that very long and strange day.

One particular moment that really sticks out in my mind as strange, as though making a day's adventure out of breaking-up with someone, wasn't strange

Chapter Two

enough. There was this one particular moment at dinner. I noticed how intensely David was staring into my eyes. It was as though he'd fallen into a trance. Incredibly drawn into me, and then all of sudden he shakes his head. As though he needed to bring himself back, back from where his mind had taken him. Back to that restaurant where we both sat...in shock. The place that would be the site of the final burial of our relationship.

I found that his actions very contradictory to what he said to me. Our connection even in the minutes that we said or maybe I should say, " were trying" to say our good-byes was as intense as our very first encounter.

...even more goodbyes!

While still in the throws of dealing with the break-up the century...at least from my stand-point, I was also dealing with another kind of break-up, my career with the fashion industry. I worked in the fashion business prior to meeting David, and both simultaneously and without proper notice came to an unwelcoming end.

During my short but illustrious (haha) career in the fashion industry. I had chosen to pursue several different types of positions. One of those positions was as a fashion coordinator in the visual department for some major retailers in the city of Chicago.

I LOVED it! I LOVE just being around creative people.

What I didn't realize...until I really started working in

the field was all the different career options that were out there. Sometimes you really don't know about all of the possible interesting options, until you get out there and start experiencing life.

One of the constant running themes in my life is that I always try to capture and discover the "road less traveled." This time it actually found me. I was working on the main floor of Marshall Field's (the store's name at that time) as a visual artist, when I was approached by this woman. She had been in before and noticed our work and she wanted to offer me a job. That job was as a photo stylist.

I had never heard of a position as a photo stylist before. So I took her card and asked her, *what company would this be for?* She said, "Playboy." I immediately pulled back. Call it prim and proper, prude, whatever. I had never heard of a career called photo styling before…but I certainly know what they photograph at Playboy…I think I'll pass…thanks!

I have to tell you though, I couldn't wait to tell David that I was approached by Playboy. I had a lot of fun with that one! Even though I was not interested the mere fact that she was presenting me with a whole new career avenue, one that I had never heard of before-was very intriguing to me. I decided to do what I LOVE to do most, and that is to do a little research and find out what was down this new avenue.

Chapter Two

...photo styling?

So what exactly is photo styling? I went up to the visual office and decided to open a phone book (life before Google), and call around to some different studios in Chicago. I proceeded to ask if they had any positions available as a photo stylist. Well, I think it was about my 10th call, when the guy on the other end, said, "Yes! *In fact I have to do a shoot coming up for this new catalog account that I just received.*" He went on to explain that it's for a new potential client and that he needed someone to help him pull it all together. He asked if I could meet with him. We did...and he offered me the job on the spot.

I don't even remember how much I got paid for the job...I'm sure that it wasn't very much. But that really didn't matter because the cool thing was, that I LOVED it. This photo styling thing was for me.

...let the styling begin!

Here I was, the first day on set. After my first initial introduction to the client, were we discussed some of the desires and expectations for his future catalog. I could tell the client was impressed, because he asked me for feedback on his current catalog.

That was the first time someone in the professional business arena asked me for my opinion. Call it intuition or just plain naivete, but I shared with him my opinions of his catalog with pure abandonment. It was really quite empowering. With zero budget and a powerful determination to make this new found direction the next chapter of my life really happen...it was time to get my "style" on.

I really enjoyed being in charge of finding everything needed to create this catalog. From creating the hair and make-up, to finding the appropriate props and of course styling the clothes. Basically, I created the entire overall look of the shot. I even had the final say on the print production side. I was so very proud of my work; it just flowed with pure abandon. And when it was all completed, I decided to shop it around to some major photo studios in the Chicago area.

With my new catalog creation in hand, I soon landed my very first full-time position as fashion photo stylist. I spent two years working as a fashion stylist, then moved on to home styling. In fact, another moment of destiny soon would come calling. It occurred when I was on set. I had received a phone call for another opportunity out of the blue. This is how I feel real opportunities occur...they come to you! Either way, she had heard about me from one of my old bosses at Marshall Fields and was calling to offer me a job with Victoria's Secret. As a regional mid-west visual coordinator.

She heard good things about me and wanted to know if I would be interested in an immediate position as a regional coordinator for Illinois thru Texas. I was very interested. As soon as I gave my notice at the studio, I found myself flying off from one VS store to another. All of this without signing any new employee paperwork. Basically, I was thrown into the belly of the beast without even realizing what I was walking into. Arriving at stores in the middle of the night. Working. Then *maybe* going back to the hotel for some sleep. It got old very quick. And since I was flying most of the time, and away from David a lot, I felt that he was quickly growing restless with my new job. Along with his restlessness, and some major issues going on behind the scenes at VS. It was just a matter of a short time, that both were gone.

Yep...first the job, then David, now everything I felt that defined me, was gone. I was no longer David's girlfriend/potential fiancee nor a fashion coordinator because I got FIRED! I felt lost. I had no career, no man, no life. So who the hell am I? I was nothing but a bucket full of self-pity and tears. I needed to get a handle on this shit...and this shit was my life.

While in the process of trying to turn the page to the next chapter. I decided, that changes were needed all across the board. I needed to reinvent myself.

First, I will start on the outside, typical...that's the easy part! Even though I needed a complete life makeover, I first started with the way I looked. I had found this picture of an actress with her platinum blonde hair, black eyeliner, and classic red lips. I thought that she looked classic, regal and mysterious all at the same time.

I wanted to be all of those things. So…let the metamorphosis begin.

…because it's what's inside that really matters, right?

Looking back at all of the things that I did during those times to try to "fix" myself, what I really needed to do was find the answers to some major general life questions. With that said…I sought to find those answers. And in that search, some of the things that I had touched upon were a little crazy and a lot were out of the box. I can easily say that it was an interesting ride… and it still is.

Lesson Learned: When *stepping out of the emotions of the moment and the craziness of life…just allow the dust to settle a little. It's amazing to see how everything usually works out for the best. As much as I hate to say it, everything does happen for a reason…it really does. You just need to gather some patience (very difficult for me) and wait and to see what the outcome is.*

Note To Self

Note To Self

Note To Self

CHAPTER THREE

Choosing to Write My Own Story...

Starting over may seem scary to most. It was essential for my survival. My career was in the toilet and the first thing I needed to do was find a job. I worked as a freelance photo-stylist, while also bartending at night. During those years of "self-discovery," the bar jobs were perhaps not the best choice, but I made great money, and my days were free to explore and reinvent myself.

Explore that's exactly what I did. Some of "my explorations" were things that others might even find just a little left of crazy. Such as past life regression, astrological readings. I think that Astrology, Numerology, understanding Law of Attraction are all quite fascinating. One doesn't have to live their life by it, but having a chart done is really quite interesting. I wish a lot more people would be a little more open to it, and not think of it as weird or sacrilegious.

In fact, a short time after the now "infamous" breakup, I went to a well-known Chicago Astrologer and she did a chart on me. For those who don't know what that means, it's when they take your day, time, and location of birth and do a complete chart of the planet's positions. At that time, she said that if David and I did not come together, that there would be a possibility in 20 years. Back then, that was not what I wanted to hear. I was just thinking who the *hell* cares about 20 years from now, how about now?

Spoiler Alert!!! Ironically here we are 20 years later and I did see him again! **Maybe just for a moment**, but still very interesting. Sometimes not everything in life is black and white…you might need to allow a little gray to seep in once in a while.

Whatever one may think about alternative thinking or esoteric arts. This whole mind/body connection perspective is what really changed my life. I truly believe now that life is far more than birth, existence, then dying. I know some may have a hard time relating to alternative thinking, but it was the height of the New Age movement in the 90's, and I was hooked. Today, I believe that using only your 5 senses is very limiting. One really should be open to the 6th sense too…intuition. Try to remain open and embrace how the mind can alter and affect positively or negatively on the body.

This whole philosophy started when I read the book Celestine Prophecy. In the first chapter of this book the author discusses the prophecies. The very first one is… *that everything happens for a reason in your life and that there really is no such thing as coincidence.* These very simple philosophies in this book helped me to see my world in a much broader perspective. It was as though it gave more depth to the moments and the events that happen in life. I like to think of those moments or events like musical notes on a sheet of music that compiles after time, creating a beautiful symphony upon completion. Very sappy…but true!

With my new ferocious appetite for reading, along with listening and learning to tune into my intuition–which was fast becoming my favorite superpower.

I truly feel my intuition is like a rudder, that helps guide my life. Today my intuition is my leading edge, but with my new goal of trying to totally let go the proverbial steering wheel in life all together. I want to see where life brings me. It's not easy when you're a total control freak. So, instead of me forcing "it" to go the way I want it to go, or believe it *should* go. I'm just trying to sit back and enjoy the ride. Easier said then done!

I have had a lot of fun diving into so many different things back then. Those times also allowed me to discover a LOVE for traveling and discovering a new LOVE for painting. That time was all about opening my eyes and not having such a myopic view towards life. Life is so much more than goals on a paper, or getting from point "a" to point "b" in life to find comfort.

The desire to start painting didn't come until many years after the art classes that I took in college. This was probably best. Because back then I was never happy

Chapter Three

with any of the final executions of my projects. My inexperience coupled with the lack of awareness on how to find, or be open to the inspiration or free expression blinded me. Simply put, finding the courage and confidence to express myself unabashedly without fear... came with time. But really, my deepest lesson was all about letting go of perfection.

It became so obvious that my issues with perfectionism were not only affecting me personally, but it was also limiting my expression with art. Personally, I couldn't understand and still struggle with this compulsion to have everything be "*just so*." It has taken years of learning to let go. Or should I say re-programming myself to let go of self-judgment and to just relax. Trying to apply allowing and flow, and not be so obsessed with the end result. This compulsion for perfection was quite severe in my youth, and I'm so appreciative that it has subsided at least 85%. At least I'm not still ironing my socks anymore. Yeah, that bad!

The need for complete perfection stems from a deep fear of loss. Somewhere along the way, someone changed your idea "of the world" and your ability to feel safe. So, now to prevent this from happening again. One tries to keep the world in a complete state of order by obsessing over perfection to prevent and guard against chaos. When really the thing that will set us all "free," is allowing a little chaos to occur. There really is no such thing as perfectionism, just humans pretending to maintain some semblance of order.

...the artist within!

I was so drawn to start painting (no pun intended). My idea of painting was a need to just allow the paint to flow onto the canvas. With just my intuition guiding me. I didn't want too much movement of the pigment, and I still don't. It's as though I didn't want to disturb the process of the paint meeting the canvas. When pushing the paint about the canvas I use a palatte knife, so I can avoid brushstroke movement. Discovering this whole process has been so freeing to me. Especially when for so long I thought that paintings had to be "photo-realistic" to be correct. So, to find comfort in the reverse... has been so incredibly liberating.

I was very inspired by Matisse and Van Gogh when I first started painting. It wasn't until many years later that I noticed that the style that I was gravitating towards again and again for my own self-expression, was Fauvism. I just LOVE the full spectrum and vivid expressionistic color choices. The paint color choices are right from the tube very little if any color combining. This application or style, is so basic and primitive. LOVE!

Painting for me is like a meditation, I try to never sketch or preplan to much before I start. With that said, yes I do have an idea at the beginning of the direction that I want each canvas to go. But there have been many times where even that has changed dramatically by the end. My lesson from my art...**is to always re-**

mind me to get out of my head more, and to follow my heart.**

The whole process of how I even found my style came while watching a TV commercial, believe it or not. It's amazing how one finds inspiration. You see, this commercial had a teacher walking up and down the aisles of a class in session stating the following, "You must stay in the lines…you must stay in the lines." Then you see this little girl sitting at her desk and coloring all over the piece of paper, with no control or desire to stay in the lines. **Because she was doing it her way**! For me, it was as though the clouds parted and the heavens spoke to me. What? She DID NOT care about what the teacher thought or found acceptable. She was totally in her own zone. That's when it hit me: *you mean it was okay to go against the establishment of the norm and do what you want to do?*

That commercial gave me the permission and the inspiration to allow my own vision. Slowly I learned to unblock and fight the vicious **dragon** of perfection allowing me the ability to create. The struggle of letting go of any inner judgment when it came to my paintings-was incredibly freeing.

Another very pivotal moment of unblocking my artistic expression came when I was going to take a class with a friend of mine. I was completely unaware that I was about to come face-to-face with the very ugly truth of how deep my own self-judgment truly was.

In this class, we were all given a black piece of paper

and a white pencil with no eraser. After we all started, I felt as though I made a mistake and I wanted to erase it. Of course, there were no erasers on the end of the pencil. So, I walked up to the teacher and asked her if I could please have another piece of paper. She said, "NO!"

"What...no?" I just paid you good money for this stupid class, now give me another piece of paper! I didn't say that...but boy I sure was thinking that! She stated to me very calmly...as I was internally raging..."Just turn the paper over." What? She has obviously lost her mind and knows nothing of my insane issues of perfection. If I turned the paper over there would be a mistake on the other side. That would not be acceptable nor good enough for me...at all!

Now let's take a moment...

And ask the congregation to please rise up and pray for this child. Because she has gone and lost her mind over a stupid piece of paper.

So resentfully...I went back to my seat. I felt like I was back in the third grade again and that I should be stomping my feet all the way back to my chair. But, I did as I was told. At least I tried. When I went back to my seat and turned the paper over, I knew that there was a mistake on the other side. I really did try to create something, but I felt like I was just faking it. All I really wanted to do was just run out of that classroom.

Finally, we all broke for lunch. Some stayed in the classroom to finish up their work before lunch. I just sat

Chapter Three

there thinking *when are we going home…or how fast can I make a break for the door?*

Minutes ticked by like hours, the lunch break was now over. And for those who needed to have more time to finish their work, they took some extra final minutes. **Would the agony ever end!?!** I felt that this particular class was one of the longest days of my life. Then all of a sudden we got even more wonderful news…the instructor would be posting the art work for everyone to see and critique. **OK, I'm going to DIE!** Are you serious…as though my life was not painful enough in that moment…now everybody is going to be looking at my dreadful expression on paper!

Don't laugh, but I physically left the room crying and had a very difficult time returning. Do you think it brought up some issues of the totally unnecessary, never possible, and emotionally destructive, dysfunction of PERFECTION? Just a little bit! Deep breath in, deep breath out! Needless to say I survived the day, barely. Whoever said that the path to awareness, healing, and creativity is easy?

…build it and it will come together, sooner or later!

After that, or maybe because of that, I still felt such a need to paint. My process to start was a lot like the movie *Close Encounters,* where everybody starts creating this volcano like shape out of everything, for reasons that you really don't know about until you reach the end of the movie.

Typical. Why can't we know the outcome of situations first? Maybe then we all would try a little harder. So like those in the movie…I just started. Very rough at the beginning, but I really liked what I was starting to see on the canvas. Gradually I was finding my vision.

In fact, I remember one of my first attempts, I wanted to have this much needed texture that I had envisioned, so, I mixed a bucket of *Plaster-of-Paris* and started slathering it all over the canvas. Only to wake the next morning to find it all over the floor. Okay, that would never work…on to the next idea.

My biggest obstacle when painting was myself. Judgment and the ability to let go of the fear of what other people will think of your creation will always be your biggest obstacle in life. It will be your job to override those fears After what felt like a very painful process of finding the right avenue of expression for me. I was starting to stockpile quite a few paintings. By stockpile, we're talking about 20. I really thought that amount was getting to be to much. Never realizing that some artists do hundreds before they even feel ready to show a small portion of them. See naïvete really can be a good thing!

Though I have reworked several of my earlier pieces, the most important thing was that I knew I had found my vision. Like life, I needed to fine-tune my original desired vision…which took years. But a day would come…where I would find out that my paintings **would be desired by others**. Enough so, that I would eventually sell about six (when I only had about 20 to begin with), and two even went into print production. No greater compliment to any artist…than to sell their art.

The whole experience of having my art out for the world to see, was an out-of-body experience. Especially, with having so many hang ups to start out with, on what "I" classified as right or wrong. The end result has truly been a gift. Reminding me to just allow and see what happens instead of trying to follow some sort of "norm" or status quo of what others may deem as acceptable.

This whole concept of living up to other peoples applied perceptions is everything that I'm not! Take creativity, many think that they need to do to follow some sort of applied program or application to be creative. Creativity is not a matter of a system or following a guideline. Following an "ABC" set of directions will not lead to creativity. That would be true for "Paint by Numbers," but not for finding your creative flow. Most people who try, or say that they cannot create. I feel are just suffering from a little "creative congestion." Or worse yet…some idea of perfection that is based in fear of expression and judgment by others.

If no one is to see the music that I have composed, at least I have seen how beautiful the melody is to my eyes.
DAKINI

For many years I never signed my canvases after I completed them. I never felt that my birth name held the power that I needed evoke for my artwork. One day while reading the book Women Who Run with Wolves, the name DAKINI jumped off the page at me. It was taken from the Tibetan name for the Goddess of Creativity, I have been signing with that name ever since I found it.

Update: Since finishing this book at this time I'm now considering using my birth name...spelled a little differently as my signature. Perhaps, after all, I have experienced in life I now feel the power and strength of my given name.

In Memory of...

Before I close out this chapter on healing, surrendering, and creativity, I would LOVE to tell you about my Father. He was the first person in my life that had an artistic vision. I felt that he was truly talented, maybe because he was my Father.

Richard W. Kueker
Editor, Photographer, Father

I used to think that my issues of perfectionism in my art stemmed from my father's career. He was a professional at photography and worked for many years as an editor for CBS news in the Chicago area. I always thought that true art should be photo-realistic, and that it must be perfect to be correct.

Perfection, is what I saw in my Father's photographs. My Dad was very talented, but he never felt that his work was exceptional. At least that was my perception of him, from what I can remember of our conversations as a child. I really looked up to him, though he passed away from a heart attack while playing golf when I was only 18 years old. I truly wish that I would have gotten to know him better as an adult. That is a loss you never recover from. I learned to adjust, creating a new normal, as we all did in our family after his death. Except for my Mom; she was destroyed by his death. But she found some comfort knowing that he died doing something that he LOVED, and not at work. That was one of the most difficult times in my life.

It was my Dad who gave me my first compliment and nod to my possible budding creative future by saying something that might seem so small and insignificant to others, but was very important to me simply because he was...my Dad.

One Christmas, I went to a local mall to pick up some presents for my family and I selected a tie for my Dad. When he received it, he sincerely told me how good my taste was in selecting that particular one for him. This was unusual because my family was not really known for their demonstrative show of emotions. Plus, my Father was an extremely particular dresser, very meticulous, so, it made me proud that he not only thought I had good taste, but he actually wore the tie to work. That is one of my most favorite memories of him.

Lesson Learned: *Healing is a mandatory step in life...I just didn't realize that it can take a lifetime of experiences to show you how far you have come in the healing process. Once* *again my issue with patience. I was always hoping that you can "fix" everything in a weekend or a special home study program... for $159.99 with FREE shipping and handling. No...unfortunately you need to just show up and do the work.*

Chapter Three

Note To Self

Note To Self

Note To Self

CHAPTER FOUR

Somewhere in Time...

After my break-up with David I obviously needed time to heal. The path to healing started with my desire to physically change my look. Then came the esoteric direction, with questions like, "Was this destined?" Then came the emotional layer. Layer after layer, I wanted to know who I was, not some "concept" of what I thought I should be.

The breakup is what really helped me to recognize all of the issues I never dealt with, before David. So, if anything I really need to thank you David. It was because of our breakup that I'm the woman I am today. And as we both know now our break up was the best thing for both of us.

But I digress and I need to get back to the subject matter of this chapter and that is to tell you about one of the wildest experiences I ever had in my travels of healing and personal discovery.

...you don't always need the actual time machine.

At that time it seemed that metaphysical practices and philosophies were all the rage! Someone had told me about past-life regression, and I really wanted to try it. I knew nothing of *past-life therapy, nor* how it was going to help me, but, I was willing to learn all about it. I was a sponge back then. The world was serving up platter after platter, of self-exploration and I was hungry.

A friend of mine gave me a lead. I called, made an appointment and even though I was little skeptical, okay, a lot skeptical. I was all in! At the same time, I was also thinking what the hell does past life therapy have to do with healing and needing answers to current day issues? I had no clue, I was just following the road, and the road lead me there...metaphorically speaking.

Appointment day had arrived. I soon found myself in this therapist's office. It was the very traditional, "lay on the couch" and tell me what's on your mind kind of situation. I didn't know what else I was expecting to happen...but it was kind of exciting. So, the session began with listening to some music and getting very relaxed. Then the instructor starts asking you some questions. And within no time, my body felt very heavy and extremely relaxed.

Within moments these images started exploding in my mind's eye. First, it seemed as though I was in the 1800's. I was viewing what felt like the back of a covered wagon. And as I was walking behind it, I noticed that I was barefoot, and wearing a long cotton flower print dress. The waist-tall grass was all around me. But then nothing. The vision went pitch black. The instructor felt that maybe I had been killed. So, she asked me to go back even further. The next thing I knew I'm standing in a garden and I'm painting. And what seems like a footman or a butler comes up to me and states, "Lady Katherine you need to get ready for tonight, the guests will be arriving shortly."

It was circa 1700's, and the gowns were full and opulent. It seemed that all one did for a majority of their day, was get ready for special events. Your makeup and then your hair. Let's talk about that hair for a minute. It was huge, like the dresses. The dress was amazing: yards and yards of fabric. I'm pretty sure that someone could hide a small car under one of those skirts, if they wanted to. Oh wait, no cars yet. Okay, continuing on. The dress was a beautiful butter cream yellow, with white lace trim. Yards and yards of opulence, all against my raven hair.

My next flash was two children playing. They were running down a hallway with sticks that had ribbons attached to them. The hallway was magnificent. It was filled with large oversized paintings and mirrors. The children seemed like distant cousins maybe a niece or a nephew to me. Then, I flashed to a party scene. People were rushing about. Champagne is flowing. I'm standing in what appears to be a receiving line. There are

Chapter Four

people waiting to meet us, mainly waiting to meet my Father.

At one point I looked up and I remembered saying to myself **he's here,** Jean-Paul. He is so beautiful to me; tall, dark hair, young and very fit. Wearing what seems to be a uniform, with gold braiding on his shoulders. So masculine, so strong, with his quiet strength that he carries. He's the type of man that just walks into a room and owns it, never needing to be the center of attention. That's what I find so irresistible.

I act as though I don't even know him, and that he means nothing to me. But the truth is, he makes me weak with desire, and filled with vulnerability. I feel him staring at me, as I pretend that I don't even notice him. When in reality, it's all I can do to stop myself from yearning to be in his arms again.

All of a sudden there is this feeling that we're together at last, the familiar sense of knowing. I'm safe...safe in his arms. Peace comes over me, when we're together. We were dancing, more like floating through the room. I was transcended. We danced and talked, and then as soon as it began, it was over.

The next flash I had, I'm talking to my Father and he is very upset with me. Telling me that I shouldn't even consider communicating with this man. Telling me the reason, *"Because he's not of our same social level."* As much as I begged and pleaded with him, there was no convincing my Father.

After that flashback or whatever you want to call these

images that kept flashing into my mind's-eye, the images just seemed to break up or get cloudy.

I do need to tell you that if you have never experienced having a past life regression before, you really should try it...it's pretty cool! It's very difficult to explain the experience. But I can use phrases like, *it's like you're watching a movie.* Then there were moments when you actually felt as though I was *in the movie.* The sensation of this experience can never be fully explained or conceptualized unless you experience it.

Getting back to these visions: The party is now over, and it feels as though time is ticking by and I am waiting and waiting. But waiting for what? Then I make the statement, *"When will he be here?"* Images appear of a courtyard with this long vestibule for arriving carriages.

The weather changes from being sunny to raining, and then it's snowing. Repeating faster and faster. It was as though time was passing; days, months, and what even feels like years are going by.

Then finally, that feeling of peace arrives again. What is this coming over me like this...or who is this? François, a new man? I'm not sure...is it the same man or a different man? If it the same man, then why do I call him by another name? I don't really know? But that same sense of splendor washes over me. Along with a knowing and a recognition.

When you're having these flashes it's not like you can stop and ask a lot of questions, the images just keep coming.

Chapter Four

With the confusion on whether this is Jean Paul or is this a new man, François? Or, is the the same person? Jean Paul is his first name and Francois is last name? Though it really didn't seem to matter. Because whoever it is, there is the most wonderful feeling of familiarity in his presence.

Do you know what I mean about that feeling? It's like when you first meet someone and immediately you feel this insane and instantaneous very deep connection between the two of you.

One of the last visions that I had while I was in this past life regression, takes place in a room that feels like a bedroom. I'm in a chair sitting by a fireplace. I'm an old woman now, and my husband is in bed. I watch over him, while he takes his last breaths. We're together at last. Until the end of our lives. Until our next lifetime together.

I know a lot people really cannot possibly relate to this whole past-life stuff. But, let me make this very clear. After experiencing this past life regression, and having another unusual experience occur to me when I was on a trip to Europe...my mind is definitely open!

The experience that I'm referring to happened when I was heading to Paris for the first time. In fact this particular trip really helped me solidify that there might be more to this "one lifetime and you're done concept". Which tends to be what the majority of others think.

...bonjour Paris!

I was so excited, it was my first trip to Europe. I didn't really know what to expect, and I'm so glad that I went solo the first time. Mainly, because I wanted to discover it on my own, first. To be in touch with what I was feeling and experiencing, without worrying too much about the needs of other people. From the moment I stepped off the plane, and into that airport there was such a feeling of calm and familiarity that came over me. No fear or worry about how I was going to navigate a country where I didn't even speak the language.

In fact, what I experienced was just the opposite; a total sense of comfort. Absolutely no anxiety or trepidation at all. When I arrived it really felt like I had been there before. It could have been me just me blowing the whole thing out of proportion, but the feeling was undeniable. The ability to know where I was, and if I walked in this direction or that direction, that I soon will be at the Louvre. Without really studying a map at all. And when I returned to Paris for the second time with some friends-I didn't have any of those same initial feelings at all.

But no matter what one believes in life. Some people just might not be sensitive enough nor open enough to embrace a lot of the serendipitous aspects of life. I have been known for, and teased about my awareness and need for signs. Yes, I know that sometimes a STOP sign, is just a STOP sign. But personally, I feel that

Chapter Four

those "signs" are occurring all around us. Showing us the way, to remind us that we're not alone.

There are those that believe that signs are the universe's way of answering us back on our truest wishes. Letting us know that they're working on those wishes. We just have to be open enough to see them...without judgment.

Case in point: There was a time when I was walking my dog around the mall where I had my shop. And I happened to notice in one of empty store fronts there was some original pieces of art that were placed on easels. Just one of the ways that the mall owners like to use the space in between lease occupancies. Being an artist, I took a moment to glance in at the art. I happened to glance down at the artist's signature. Believe it or not, the artist had the exact last name of David. Now, David's last name is very common in his country. But not at all here in the United States. Another one of those crazy coincidences? Who knows!

Lesson Learned: *Don't be afraid of the road less traveled...sometimes the roads that are the least traveled are the most exciting ones. In other words...never settle for what others find acceptable.*

Note To Self

Note To Self

Note To Self

Note To Self

CHAPTER FIVE

Can I get you a Cocktail?

I have kept many journals throughout the years, but one day I decided to burn them all, for a reason that I really can't articulate. It just felt right. Burning them almost felt as though I was subconsciously performing some sort of ritual to prevent the past from repeating. Who knows? Those journals were just a simple place for me to go, and to **express** my stories of LOVE's and life's conundrums.

Whatever avenue I use to express my desired visions in life, like this one right now, in writing this book, my objective was never to master or excel at the art of writing. This book maybe riddled with poor grammar and dangling participles (whatever that means). How about my blatant use of adverbs? Yeah, take that grammar police. My life is not about living up to other people's concepts. This book is legible, and I feel that I have expressed my opinion, mistakes and all! Job well done!

I tried. I wish more people would just, try. I think we would see a lot more untethered art out in the world today if that was true. I never set out to be an award-winning author.

Same as when I paint-I write and paint for me. Never Got The Memo, was a very difficult project for me. I wanted to put my story in words. A story of a great LOVE. The hardest part was connecting the dots of past to the present without boring you with every minor detail of my life. There will be many stories that will go untold: a girl needs a little mystery. I'm just enjoying the discovery of another way to express my own individual "free-spirit" voice.

But getting back to the now embers of past journals. One of those "lost stories" was about a moment that I had seen David, about 4 to 5 years approximately after we broke up.

...what are the chances?

It was a cool spring day, and the Chicago winter's snow had not completely melted. I was working as a manager at a natural skin care center. In a blink of an eye as I had glanced up from my desk and I saw a familiar reflection in the mirror. I couldn't believe what I had seen. It was his car. When I saw the license plate, which had his name on it-I thought to myself...OMG! That's him! I couldn't believe what I was seeing...what were the chances?

His car was unmistakable. I would know it anywhere.

Probably because I helped David bring it back to Chicago from the east coast. After he bought it on the gray market in Germany. The experience that we both had- or maybe I should say, that I had while bringing that car back home-was crazy. Let's just say that it was a little nerve-racking as he ripped over and around mountains testing out his new toy on our way back to Illinois.

The memory of bringing that car back to Chicago is forever seared into my brain. It was a dark rainy evening. The only light seemed to be coming from the luminescent reflection of the oncoming car's headlights off the raindrops on my windshield. We were driving in separate cars, on back country roads-the night he pushed his new car and my patience to the limit.

I followed closely behind him the entire way back, as David ripped around those steep mountain roads, taking curves like he did when he first drove it on the Autobahn in Germany. At one point we pulled over and I pleaded with him to please slow down. I had been so mad in that moment, that the memory of that car is forever seared in my mind. So, to see that car again, brought me right back to those mountains, the rain, and of course, him!

As I looked up and saw David running up to a storefront next to the clinic, I knew that I needed to get his attention. So I waited until he got a little closer I said, *"David, David is that you?"* He came over and gave me a hug, and we proceeded to make small talk.

I knew that he was now married and I decided to ask

Chapter Five

him...in fact I rather just blurted it out. *"I hope that you are happy?"* I didn't mean it to sound salty or snarky in any way at all. In fact, I think I even threw in a head tilt too...just to add a little more softness to the question.

As we both stood there, I was completely oblivious to anything and anyone around except him. We continued to make small talk, and I decided to ask him again, *"Are you happy?"* Once again he didn't reply. I don't know if he just chose not to answer me, but I found some comfort in his non-answer. Or maybe he just didn't know to tell me that he had found happiness after all. Our lives were obviously have very separate and different now. I wished him well and returned to where I was working.

...so whats next?

Back then I was growing bored and restless of those filler "odd" jobs, and I had this intense desire to start my own business. The first business that I created was with my sister Linda. It was a small gift business, a pop-up site at Christmas at a local mall. My sister was the money end, and excellent at it. I designed and created all of the merchandise. It only lasted one holiday season but it truly did whet my appetite for a desire to create something more permanent of my own one day.

Some years later I created Before and After's. This business idea was conceived from combining my LOVE of home décor, along with my expertise in set styling.

I chose to market it to the private home owner, to help them recreate a room or rooms in their home in hopes of elevating their current look and taking it to the next level.

Many consumers really want their own fingerprint in their homes. They're just not always sure of the proper style direction, color or layout that would be best. They just need someone to help them cultivate and bring out their own desired vision correctly, and most importantly, economically.

Homes I believe are our sanctuaries, the place that should **welcome** us. Especially, when the day is done. A place where we find comfort, peace, and safety. No matter the budget or what we as designer's feel is the current appropriate trend, I feel that everyone's homes deserves to be treated with respect and given a chance to come alive.

Even though I LOVED starting and owning my businesses at times; money was tight. And because I like to have nice things-I took a position as a bartender at a local high-end martini lounge-Martini's were all the rage. This particular place was "the place to be and work." The club was called the Living Place.

It was owned by a man named Antonio Marino and I found him fascinating, charming, smart, friendly, and serious, all at the same time. I'm pretty sure that those who crossed him, never forgot him. My days there were very, very prosperous.

Every night that I was there brought a unique level of

Chapter Five

excitement. Antonio was a good boss and I really enjoyed working for him. Believe me, I have worked for a lot of "jack holes" in my time. Antonio, was tough, but always fair. Maybe this was just my perspective, but I don't think that I was the only employee who felt that way. I truly feel that a lot of the employees felt a connection to him. Good or bad they respected the man.

I was assigned to one of the worst bars on the main floor. Looking back at that situation now, I could have been forced to work at one of the upstairs bars, so I guess it was fine. But boy, did I bitch when I first started. So there I was, buried behind all of these plants at this bar right by the main entrance. After I stopped feeling sorry for myself. I started to think, if I just moved all of these plants that are blocking me from the people that are walking in the front door. I could ask those same people if...*I could get them a cocktail.* I would be like a Walmart greeter for alcoholic beverages, in a much cooler atmosphere!

When people first arrive at a new club, they're usually a little nervous. Perhaps they may need a little "liquid courage?" That was one of the smartest things I had ever done. I took what I thought were lemons, and made lemonade out of it. Very good and expensive lemonade. Maybe Antonio saw what I did and it made an impression on him. Because he took very good care of me; I always felt that he looked out for me.

Not everyone felt same way I did about him. In fact, one particular bartender that I worked with, always

LOVED to interject this little statement when Antonio would go around and pass out money *(side tip)* to us. "Well you know if you accept that...you now know that he owns you!"

I understood where she was coming from, but that never stopped her from taking his side tips. In fact, she even chose to have her wedding at The Living Place. One of the few that they ever hosted there. So, as far as being "owned?" Sometimes that's the price we pay for things that we want. Like a great price for a sit-down dinner for your wedding...right Kitty Cat.

This idea of him passing out money was true, he did take very good care of us. He even gave us all a Christmas bonus. Which really was unheard of in the bar business. He was very generous boss. The club was his side hustle, his main business, was as the owner of one the largest produce distribution centers in Chicago, if not the country.

Another great *Antonioism,* was when he heard you were going to Las Vegas, he would give you some money and ask you to bet it for him. Obviously knowing that everybody would either bet it, and then keep the money, or just have fun with the extra cash. And I'm sure that's what his original intention was all along for everyone. When some friends and I decided we were going to Vegas, because you have to go at least once in your life-yes, he gave me some money, but I decided that I would do something a little different with it.

When I first arrived there, I immediately placed a bet,

Chapter Five

and I told myself if I won I would return the money... and that's exactly what happened. I arrived back home I told him that I have something for him from Vegas, and when I pulled out the money and gave it back to him... the look on his face was priceless.

Now, before all of you fall off your chair and say why!?! I wanted to, I leave being typical and obvious for everyone else. And yes the obvious thing would have been to just say thank you, and then say that I lost the bet. I assure you I was probably the only one that ever brought the money back to him.

But this is where reality stepped in. When I went to hand him back the money-yes, I LOVED the look on his face as I was returning it-but I was so greatly disappointed when he kept it. I'd wanted him to say, *"No you keep it, you won it!"* Moral of the story...watch how high you put someone on a pedestal because that fall... is a tough one.

After 5 years at the Living Place, I left for a very good reason. I decided to move to California. Antonio made a heavy impression on me. Maybe those who read this and know of him may have had a different experience, but he taught me some valuable lessons as a business owner.

First, always respect those who take care of you. Second, you' re never too powerful to wash your own dishes, especially when no one else can. And the most important lesson of all, *how to take someone to the next level.*

Antonio made that comment to me when he left LP, which happened to be right around the same time that I was leaving, because he had sold the club. At first, I really didn't know what he had meant by "taking someone to next level". Now, with some life experience behind me, I may have a better idea. It may not be his definition-but this one is mine.

Finding that something special in someone else and allowing them to be who they are, but also giving them boundaries and wings at the same time. People like to be acknowledged, heard, and most important of all...validated.

Thanks, Antonio...it was a pleasure!

Note To Self

Note To Self

Note To Self

CHAPTER SIX

Following Your Heart...

I have met and dated the good, the bad, and the ones that made me say, "W*hat the F&%# was I thinking!?!*" There have even been a choice few that I didn't even give a chance at all. Perhaps to my loss, and now regret. My romances were limiting, frustrating and fleeting. The ability to find that right "one" and to *know at first sight (again),* that he is the one that I wish to spend my life with, has been one of my greatest challenges in life.

Sure there have been times when I have felt that I had fallen under some evil spell by a wicked queen, or that there is an invisible force field surrounded me (kidding of course) but if anyone knows how to get in contact with Wonder Woman...email me.

Days turned into months, months turn into years. The usual fear of time ticking away that most women are concerned with, didn't have that same effect on me. For the main reason that I did not desire to have my own children. Though I would truly welcome my future husband's children and his future grandchildren.

I LOVE children, I just didn't see myself in a "Mom" role. Oddly enough, the first book that I wrote-was a children's book. I titled that book The Little Note. It's all about a musical note trying to find the courage to express himself in the world.

I know myself very well, and if I truly wanted children, I would have had children whether I was married or not. I just felt that it was not my calling in this lifetime.

Even though I always felt a slight pang of guilt whenever I made such a proclamation. Sometimes, I even feel as though I might have a dysfunctional chromosome not to desire to give birth. But that's just it, I have chosen to create...just in other ways.

I believe that raising children is an art form, for which I really don't take lightly. Being a parent takes a great amount of patience, dedication and understanding. I have watched my sister and her husband with their children, and I marvel at their strength. My sister has made a conscious choice to break the chain to how we were raised. I'm so very proud of her and how she has handled herself. They're both dedicated and LOVING parents.

...life is about learning to let go!

While writing this book I have chosen to consciously say goodbye to some people in my life. No matter what the circumstances were about I needed to dissolve those connections.

What I'm really coming to terms with, is that each individual person you invite into your life, brings in their own special dogma. Those perspectives are as unique as our own finger prints. But as long as those terms include respecting each other's values and desires...then it's all good.

When involved in a situation where your opinion and their opinion don't match up, and one of the parties involved is feeling challenged, threaten, or not heard, that's where the push back starts to happen. Push back is where we all start to fall into the abyss. The point where you either stay level-headed and present, or go into red alert-activate **Defcon One** level of protection. Sometimes exchanges happen that you later regret.

Whenever you go into defensive mode, it's not good. Because that's when you're leading with ego, and the stronger the ego...the dirtier the fight. Just so you can hold your ground, and prove everybody else wrong. It takes a very strong person to have an awareness and understanding to not buy into other people's crap, and disengage.

When it comes to confrontations no one likes them. Let's face it, we always feel like we're walking a very uncomfortable fine line when confrontations occur. That line of feeling like a doormat if you don't say something, or acting like a major bitch when you do. Confrontations are awful, that's why they should be avoided at all costs. There's never a perfect resolution. The ONLY resolution...is to walk away.

I have played both sides...and yes if feels good to puke out all of your verbal attacks in the moment, but afterwards, it feels like you're just trying to justify yourself to others. Trying to convince them of your standpoint, of why you overreacted. When in reality all that really happened-was that you both walked away feeling defeated and reduced. You may think you got the upper hand by being defensive and holding your ground, but you really didn't. The only thing you did was emotionally exhaust yourself.

This is what separates the girls from the women, and the boys from the men. Why? Because whenever you're involved in a situation where you feel that you have to defend your position, and fight for personal justification. Then it's just an ego blood bath. Learn to disengage. Finding the balance between needing to retreat, and the need to strike out and defend...that's where maturity lives.

I used to pride myself on a good verbal battle, but lately...that fight has long left the building.

But-I will still always enjoy a good verbal foreplay session.

To me that is a when there is this insane mutual intellectual connection combined with a lot of under lining sexual chemistry. I LOVE the whole "art" of seduction or suggestion. It's all about carrying yourself without complete exposure. That mystique is so very intoxicating to me. There have been very few men that I have met in my life that could really handle a good verbal repartee, but they will forever remain-unforgettable.

I truly enjoy the entire process of discovering someone else's perspective in the world. It's like unwrapping a gift really slow. Whether it's a lover or just someone that I like to hang out with. Meeting people and discovering how they see the world, I find it truly fascinating. We all bring such diverse opinions and desires to the table, and we're not always going to agree...but that's okay.

Being a FREE-SPIRIT, I tend to be pretty low-key. But when I have taken enough of other people's crap, or their idle BS, I'm DONE! I can be incredibly patient (with some things), but if certain situations occur and I see how incredulous another can be...I walk.

I have vacillated drastically even in my own confrontations, from reacting to withdrawing, and at times finding peace with a middle ground. I feel that the most important aspect in life is to strive for non-reaction. But boy, people might not feel comfortable with you not standing up for yourself. You might hear comments like, "Why didn't you say something?" "Are you going to let them get away with that?" If this happens to you. And you have chosen to not engage in a confrontation. Just turn to them and say, "I'm trying a different approach now. *I'm choosing me and my sanity!*" That should shut them up.

I know that all relationships are not made to be forever. Being detached from any expectations and from any desired outcome is where to be. Try to stay present and enjoy what's in the moment.

Along with this "acceptance" of letting go of desired outcomes. I also needed to learn the difference between a boundary, and having a barrier. The difference between the two has helped me evolve personally. Having barriers is when someone decides that they just do not want to talk to you, period.

Let's say that you did something wrong, and the hurt party refuses to keep the lines of communication open. In other words, he or she is choosing to turn their back, and purposefully choosing not to talk, because they're hurt. Not even stating that they need some time to heal, before they can decide how they would like to proceed. That's putting up **a barrier. Selectively choosing to push someone away. That need for drama is steeped in selfishn**ess and ego.

If someone chooses to walk away from a friendship or any type of connection after they have explained why the connection is no longer a good thing because they might have felt that the connection was NOT rooted in equal support and acknowledgment...that's having boundaries.

Accepting and respecting, are the major factors in having a good set of boundaries. Whether it's at work or in your personal life, it takes bravery and a strong sense of character to choose to walk away from a connection. It's amazing to me how many people will allow dysfunctional and abusive relationships in their life. For the pure and simple fact of needing companionship.

Lesson Learned: *During our lives, we meet so many different types of personalities. It can be very difficult to navigate through all of their varied egos. I can be a little more open to trust then others at first. But don't get that twisted, if I choose to give you my heart, and you abuse it or mistreat it, we're done! NO QUESTIONS. And let me be very clear this does not pertain to minor issues and conflicts. This will occur after, either trying to communicate(using boundaries not barriers) or severe interactions. Because I'm a person that's very comfortable in what I can offer in a connection. And yes, I do expect others to be mature and responsible for their actions too.*

Note To Self

Note To Self

Note To Self

CHAPTER SEVEN

California Bound...

For the first time in my life I was considering leaving the state that I was born and raised in. To see what new adventures could be found in California.

There is a famous phrase that goes something like this. *You're either running from something or you're running to something.* In this case it might be the latter. But if I could really choose...*I would like to take a third option Alex-for the true daily double (Jeopardy).* And that third option is what I would like to call the "weigh stations" of life. Yep, I like that. The weigh station's of life. Weigh stations are those areas where the trucker's need to pull off the road so they can have their load checked to see if it's safe for them to keep moving forward on their desired path.

California was one of those weigh stations in my life. A time where I needed to pull off the road in my journey to do a self-check of where I have been, and where I would like to go.

While having life goals, I had to learn how to be really detached from the end results. It's difficult to dream, put things in action, and then not care about what happens to those dreams. In fact, this is another aspect of life that's still very challenging for me, waiting patiently. Unfortunately, I like to push the river.

...sign, sign, everywhere a sign!

While I was still trying to decide if I wanted to move to California. I had asked for a sign to help me to figure out what to do. It was raining hard that day. The thunder was crashing hard. Distracting me.? Or maybe trying to get my attention. "*Should I move to California?*"

At one point, the rain had stopped. So I decided to step outside, and as I looked up, totally not expecting anything. The most magnificent double rainbow appeared.

I had never seen a double rainbow before and in that moment...I felt that was my answer. For all you fatalists and realists out there, that's how I feel signs show up in our life. Subtly. It's just up to us to choose to see them as signs...or not.

With that said, the house was packed, and everything went into a storage. The final step was buying a new car, an SUV. I was now ready to see what was in California. My friends just couldn't believe that I was doing this myself. My only thought was, why not? Are *we NOT supposed to do things in life just because we don't have someone to do it with?*

When being asked aren't you afraid? I don't know why, but when I tried to think of a response back. My first thoughts were always about not comprehending a fear that others were attaching to trying something new and different. Oddly, when I was asked this question, my first thoughts even reflected back to my first days of getting behind the wheel of a car, and how incredibly ecstatic I was to be given an avenue to advance my boundaries. It was as though someone was saying to me, "there is so much than this."

Correlating these two random situations of finding the courage to move out-of-state alone, along with learning to drive may seem obscure, but learning to drive-is something that we all must learn do on our own. Yes, at first we need to have someone else in the car that is a licensed driver, but eventually it's just you and the car, and freedom.

My days of being a new driver were filled with excitement and exploration. And now looking back on those days, quite a bit of luck too. I had very little experience behind the wheel of a car. Mainly because my Dad would never let us drive his car's. One of the most stressful and craziest moments came on a very cold and snowy January night. My Dad just got me a car, and I was on my way downtown to Chicago. I was on a very busy four lane highway, when I realized that I couldn't stop the car in time for a stoplight, due to ice on the road. I didn't know what to do, I was so extremely inexperienced. So, believe it or not I let go of the steering wheel and laid down across the front seats.

Chapter Seven

I laid there, waiting for the car to collide into something. The wait was like inertia. Then I started to realize that the car had never veered nor changed lanes. So, with no obvious sounds of an impact, I just sat up and resumed driving again. Yep...totally crazy...I know!

In fact, I must have some really good car karma, because years later I had another major weird driving situation happen. When I once again found myself on a very busy four lane road. When I noticed this car in front of me. It was driving towards me in my lane. The driver was coming towards me, and he was coming fast.

The headlights were getting bigger and brighter. Then it was as though someone or something took over my body. I was in a complete state of peace and total balance. The car seemed like it was yards from me, I just turned the steering wheel, and very calmly drove in the opposite lane, where *the other driver* should have been.

When I knew he passed me, I simply steered the car back into my original lane. That same car hit the car behind me and then went off the road into a forest of trees.

The possible severity of these two situations never really registered with me at that time. Nor, the symbolism of those moments. Though I think back now and I can't believe how calm I was, and how they're both great examples of how in life you just need to "let go" of the wheel (figuratively) and relax. Lean back, allow the flow, without reacting to life, and watch the craziness that is going on all around you while you enjoy the ride. Just NEVER do that in a moving car if you can help it!

My ability to let go of any fear, and to be open to all of the possibilities of what could happen with me traveling just wasn't even there. My first reaction to anything new, is to not invite in negative situations or difficulties that "might" occur. I really try to stay open. Unlike my early days of driving...cautious but open!

But...like all things in life. I would find out much later in my life that I wasn't completely immune to fear like I had once thought I was. I'm not talking about the type of fear, like being afraid of snakes. I'm talking about emotional fear (rational or irrational). I found out personally that FEAR can come into your life when you least expect it. And usually, it will show up when you're feeling very vulnerable.

Anxiety, interesting word, an anagram for "any exit." A point where it's mandatory to either suit up and find out what you're made-of, or find a way to escape that fear...by numbing it or pushing it away.

...on the road!

I planned to stop off at my brother Glen's house in Arizona, before eventually settling in California. Glen left to find a new direction himself several years before me. It was great seeing him, and all that he has accomplished after moving to Arizona, I'm very proud of him.

After staying with him for about a couple of weeks, I continued on to California. I relished every moment of driving. Even the moments that some might find mundane. Loving the scenery as I passed through deserts, suburban areas, and then finally arriving at the very busy urban traffic of LA. Not even realizing, that I was living out the greatest metaphoric statement there is, *it's the journey...not the destination.*

...Welcome to California!

When I finally arrived in LA, I was able to stay with a friend that I knew from back in Chicago, giving me time to see what this crazy place was all about. I wanted to explore and see if this could be a place that I would like to call home. Every day I drove around just exploring. Trying to figure out what was behind the "velvet ropes" of this place called Hollywood.

I TITLED THIS PICTURE "THE POSER, EXHIBITIONIST AND THE LOSER"...WELCOME TO CALIFORNIA!

I LOVED exploring different neighborhoods on a daily basis. I had even heard about this one particular bookstore that housed all these different scripts and much-needed contact information that I could use to do some research on the film business. Just my kind of place to do a little investigative work.

So, I located that shop and the contact information I needed. If I was going to see if this place could be a future home for me-I needed to get my foot in the door in the film business. I was hoping to use my experience from Chicago as a photo stylist in "still" photography to see if I could land a job in "film" as a set designer. My goal was to research and find those much needed contacts, to possibly make this happen.

Armed with my Chicago tenacity and a lot of determination. No correction...make that very little determination. Looking back now, I really didn't try very hard at all to see what my opportunities were "out there." I did call some of the people on the list. Some called me back and many did not. After a lot of attempts, I finally got to speak with this one woman who I believe might have even been on a board for one of the set designer's associations.

She said up front, "We don't have any opportunities at all. If you would like to be booked in Canada, we may have some opportunities up there. But either way, you're going to have to work for FREE for a while, then after you prove yourself. Things can happen." I thought, she was either a little bitter, or Gail welcome

Chapter Seven

to LA! The land where you need to be cutting, or you will get cut!

That's actually, a perfect little metaphor for this LA-LA town. Long story short, I tried to find a way into the "film" biz, but without having any major contacts (land of nepotism), and very little desire to start over, I decided to move on. Basically, I grew bored of trying... really quick. My true desire and passion was not driving me at all. Plus, I just didn't feel a connected to that whole area in general.

It wasn't until I left LA, that I realized that I actually had a major contact. But, it was too late. I was already in the car on my way to my next adventure. It was just not meant to be. Besides the gypsy in me was getting restless.

...the road was calling again!

Highway One is probably one of the most incredibly beautiful roads, possibly in the entire United States. When I drove it for the first time, making my way up to Santa Barbara, it took my breath away. I stayed long enough to experience my first earthquake, but soon the road would be calling me again.

As I climbed north on route one, I was never intimidated nor sidetracked from remembering how very exciting this whole adventure was to me. I felt so fortunate to be able to take the time out and to travel like this. I LOVE the excitement of discovering new areas that I had never seen before.

Now fast approaching Big Sur. It was just one splendor after another, so much to see and take in. The jagged cliffs, the ocean, the deceptively calm and tranquil water, with all the beautiful shades of blue-green. The roadside cliffs with their huge limbering trees, climbing off of the sides. They almost appear as paint brushes, just lightly dabbing in that day's color for the water.

All this beauty to take in, just within the coastal area alone. It was so inspiring. Literally jaw dropping after living in the flat lands, a prairie state. While working my way north I came upon a town marker. The sign read Carmel. Hey, a town I have heard of before. I thought I'd turn in and see what this little village was all about.

As I pulled into town and proceeded down Ocean Drive. Wow! It was so charming and quaint. From the moment that I turned down Ocean, I was hooked. I was so drawn to this place. The village looked like something out a fairy tale. It had a very Hansel-Gretel feel. I needed to find out what this place held for me.

Lesson Learned: *Never be afraid to try and do things or go places with just yourself...being alone is a state mind.*

Chapter Seven

Note To Self

Note To Self

Note To Self

CHAPTER EIGHT

Ruby Slippers...

Carmel, California is everything a little sea-side town should be.

From the moment I pulled into town and decided to stay, things just lined up. I instantly found this great place to live. And within days of that I found a pretty good job as an assistant to an Interior Designer in Monterey. The money wasn't exactly rolling in, so I chose to also seek part-time work.

That part-time job, was as a bartender in one of the dinner clubs at the Pebble Beach Golf Resort. That turned out to be a lot of fun! To wait on, and see all celebrities that came through there. It was pretty cool for a girl from the Midwest. I enjoyed every minute of my life in Carmel.

Carmel, the epitome of quaintness and charm. There was always things to do and places to explore. One of my favorite areas was Jane Adams Park. It had this private waterfall and turquoise lagoon. Seriously, mind-blowing. Though you could only view it from a vista above.

But I truly felt transcended when I went there. I used to go there and write, it was magical for me.

It really felt like it had everything. I can also state honestly say that it's an incredibly beautiful place...but there was still something missing. I really didn't know what it was, that created the feeling of not desiring to completely settle in and have my furniture brought out.

...*by the sea!*

When I talked to friends back home I used to tell them all about the local flavor and environment. In fact, I was joking around and called out the local policemen. And how they had one of those cars with the single sirens on top...you know the kind that Sheriff Andy Taylor used to drive.

In fact, I used to say to friends back home on the phone, "*I haven't seen Aunt Bee and Opie yet. But if I do maybe it will be time for me to go home."* I was actually being very sarcastic and just stating that, because of how small the village felt to me, but I would soon discover how important, and true those words would become.

One of my favorite experience in Carmel happened when I became fast friends with someone I worked with at Pebble Beach. She was getting her pilot's license and she had asked me if I wanted to go up in one of the Cesena's that she LOVED to fly. I thought cool, sure why not!

So the following day I met her at the local small craft airport. Carmel by air…is unbelievably beautiful. I enjoyed the scenery, as we were flying so low at times I thought the wings would brush the sides of the jagged cliffs. Her time was soon up, so she was needed to take the plane back to the airport. It was then that I noticed that she had circled the airport a couple of times. It was also then she decided to tell me that she is still *practicing her landings*! What…maybe I didn't hear her right. Did you say, **"Still practicing your landings?"**

OMG! So after four or five attempts thank "f"ing" whomever…that she was able to land that tin bucket! OMG! Yes, need to say that again. Oh, and a little background information John Denver lost his life…in a plane crash…over that same area-due to pilot error. It's quite well known that the wind current can change in a instant causing problems; especially for a novice pilot. OMG!

But we landed and that would be the first and last time I'd ever do that. What a great area for that to be

Chapter Eight

my one and only experience in a small craft airplane... especially with a pilot carrying a beginner's license.

You know, California is very interesting. As they say, it's filled with hopes and promises. A lifestyle that is unmatched in any other area. One time I went to a Halloween party of someone who designed the car for Batman. It seems that no matter what, you couldn't turn or spit without hitting some form of Hollywood. Not like I spit, but you know what I mean. There was a time when I went to the grocery store in Carmel Valley and saw Doris Day!

Okay, come on...Doris Day...shopping for food. I know you need a vacuum to pick up all these names I have been dropping here. But it was true and fun for the short time that I did lived there. You have to remember... I'm just a girl from the Midwest and if I would have met the head janitor at Paramount Studios, I would have been star struck. What can I say, I'm easily impressed.

As much as I enjoyed the area, I didn't feel settled in or connected. I was completely frustrated with the ambivalence that I was experiencing. As intoxicatingly beautiful as Carmel was, something was holding me back. I became quite crazed about this decision. At the end of day, my gypsy spirit, does like to feel comfortable about having some sort of direction and a place to call home.

I'm usually very assured and determined when I want something. I'm quite confident in my steps and what I need to do to possibly achieve those things in life. But this "not knowing" is foreign to me.

One night when I was getting ready for bed, I remember saying out loud, *"Please help me to find the right answer. To know whether I should stay or go back home?"* In other words, **yes...send me a sign!**

I was very restless that night. It was about two in the morning when the phone rang. First, I thought it was a friend of mine back home calling to tease me about not being there-while they were all out. So I picked up the phone half-asleep and said, *"Hello."* The strange thing is the woman on the other end said "hello" at the same time. Then we both said it again, then again.

"OK, who is this?" She once again parrots me. *"All right, it's late, my name is Gail Kueker who is this?"* She stated, "Gail, Gail on Beach Drive?" "Yes who is this? "Gail this is your landlord, what is going on? My phone rang here(land lines)!" I replied, "S*o did mine, I think both of our phones rang at the same time."* She did not understand that statement at all. She then asked me if everything was okay with the apartment and I said, *"Yes, everything is fine."* I continued on by saying, *"Listen I need to hang up...I do need to talk to you, but I will call you another time."* After that, we both hung up, and I knew what my answer was...**I was going home**!

As soon as I made that proclamation out loud, I felt a huge weight fall off my shoulders. That's when I knew that I had made the right decision. I trusted myself!

As we all know Dorothy (from the Wizard of OZ),

Chapter Eight

discovered that she had the ability to decide when to go home the whole time. Those "ruby slippers" are a great metaphor for those who question their own ability to feel confident about making their own decisions in life. Always remember that you're the "only one" that truly holds the power to know what is right when it comes to decision making. Let go, and *trust* in the outcome. Do not FEAR the unknown.

That was one of the most pivotal moments in my life and I was truly happy with my decision. So, the next day the first thing I did was call my friends and family to tell them that I was heading back to Illinois. I was ready to go home!

And for those thinking that maybe a phone call in the middle of the night is just not enough of a reassurance that it would be the right direction, another very convincing "sign" occurred that very next day. I was out driving around doing errands, and as I was turning a corner...there it was on a license plate.

If you remember at the beginning of this chapter when I was explaining about the town I was living in to my friends back home? I always said...*I haven't seen Aunt "B" or Opie, yet but when I do, I know that it will be time to go home.* Well, you guessed it, there it was...as clear as day! On a license plate...B (Heart) Opie. Well, I guess I saw B and Opie now...I can go home! I LOVE life and the signs that are all around us...directing us. You just need to be aware and open to the possibilities.

...homeward bound!

It was a long and arduous drive back to Chicago, but it still felt great to be going home...it just felt right. As I entered Chicago, rounding Lake Michigan it was strange to see it again. Not in a bad way, but in a good way. Believe it or not, I found it even more beautiful than the Pacific Ocean. Go figure! Maybe I was just so happy to be home.

I needed to get settled in right away. Some friends of mine had just opened a new restaurant and they asked me to help them when I returned home. Along with helping them, I also decided to re-establish the home-styling/design consulting business that I had created before I left, *Before and After's*. Only this time I decided to rename it Finishing Touches Studio.

Lesson Learned: *Always follow your own heart and trust your own inner intuition! In fact, there is a phrase that haunted me for years. When the student is ready the teacher will* *come. Well, it took me so long to grasp the real understanding of this phrase. That we are the students and the teachers. You simply evolve in life from the "students" perspective to the "teachers." Because we're the only one that can truly give ourselves the right answers. We just need to start trusting in those answers, and more important ourselves.*

Note To Self

Note To Self

Note To Self

Note To Self

CHAPTER NINE

Following My Inner Buddha...

I always enjoyed creating and inspiring others. So, after re-establishing my business under it's new name. I was drawn for some reason to create a new product line. A novelty gift idea. I have no clue why...just once again following my own **Inner Buddha**.

The products that I produced were inspirational tee-shirts and candles. They both had contracts attached to them and those contracts were for the recipient to sign as an allegiance to themselves. Promising to discover one of the greatest mysteries of life...their true self! This is what the contract stated.

Living Authentically

- **Choose to live life with total authenticity to your soul's desire.**
- **Honor your dreams, desires, and passions in life; this must take precedence.**

- **Though this candle may burn down (or this tee shirt may fade)as the years go by, your dreams and passions will not.**
- **Understanding that living authentically means that you no longer have a desire to live up to other people's expectations.**
- **Belief and faith in your dreams are mandatory. Stay present: do not dwell on the past, nor the future.**
- **Never limit your visions; be open to the unexpected.**
- **Authenticity of your soul's music comes with the discovery of the importance of the space and fullness between the notes.**
- **Seeing is not believing: believing is seeing. Surrender to all concepts of what should be, and LOVE unconditionally.**

I feel very strongly that life is about finding your own definition of happiness and that you must follow your own personal dreams and aspirations.

It was Antonio Marino the club owner, that I had once worked for that who told me that sometimes when you achieve things in your life. That just the act of the achievement alone, can bring envy and jealousy among those you have counted as your closest friends. If it also happens to come with financial success, some may find that even more threatening and may even choose to break away from the friendship completely.

I couldn't really understand why he was telling me this, it seemed so random. Especially at that particular moment in my life. He obviously didn't know my friends and of our close connections. Unfortunately, years after he shared his sage advice, I would sadly find out how true his words were.

I would never have thought that I would have to deal with that very same issue that he brought up. The problem of having someone in my life not being 100% happy for me, with or without financial success...it just seemed so beyond reason.

...it started with a feeling and a vision!

My business was really starting to pick up and I felt that I was on the right track. Life was really going good as well, especially after taking the time to live out a gypsy lifestyle for awhile. I'm so glad that I decided to listen to my own inner desires and not worry about what others thought, when deciding to come back home.

I was loving my life and how I was designing it, especially with the decorating business (sorry about the pun). In fact, a friend of mine at the time told one of her co-workers about my business, because he was needed a interior designer, after just coming off a divorce.

His home was a blank canvas, and I was selected to help him create a new look and feel. He was basically starting from scratch. That type of project can be very exciting. This was one of my very first major projects, and I was pretty much given carte blanch to create whatever I wanted. As a designer those kind of opportunities just don't come around that often.

We were working on that design project almost daily and I found him very easy to work with. The strange part was that I kept having this nagging feeling that he needed to meet another friend of mine. So I decided to put this feeling to rest, and introduce them.

They met…and they're now married! Never question the strength of your intuition!

Lesson Learned: *Be satisfied or at peace with what is… but be eager to see what is coming.*

Note To Self

Note To Self

Note To Self

Note To Self

CHAPTER TEN

Pure LOVE in a package of a... Soft Coated Wheaten Terrier!

Sometimes life can bring you a perfect little package. Some feel that those packages come with two feet, well mine came with four paws. It was a four legged paw's of perfection-my dog Henri, a Soft Coated Wheaten Terrier!

I had just moved into this cute little cottage. I had always wanted to live in a carriage house off an estate somewhere. It always just sounded so romantic and magical. When I found this particular carriage house, it was not exactly my ideal, but it was still nice! It was located in Barrington Hills, about 45 minutes west of Chicago. Buried deep in the greenery of wisteria-covered trellis's and dew-dripping peonies. With it's rolling lawns, this particular carriage house had a long driveway that carried you through a porte-cochere up to the cottage that had two patios, one screened in and the other one over looked a small lake in the back. I was LOVING my life and everything it was bringing, I was very busy with my design business, along with freelancing every once in a while as a photo stylist. Life was really good, and I felt so full, LOVE was a constant presence in my life.

I will never forget this one day, as I was pulling out of that long driveway. I remember thanking the universe for all of the blessings that had come into my life. Now more than ever I really feel that you have to be in total appreciation not just for the big moments, but even the smallest of moments that occur in life too. This is the "nirvana" in life…honoring the simplicity of life.

Getting back to my four-legged package of pure LOVE! I saw Henri for the first time shortly before the 4th of July weekend in 2005. This dog, at a moment's notice, captured my heart without me even realizing it. I was leaving for the holiday weekend, flying out to see my sister and her family, living in Connecticut. While I was out there, I couldn't get this dog out of my head. Me, of all people, I was the last person in the world who would ever be interested in owning a dog!

I always thought dogs were cute, I just felt that my lifestyle was never conducive to properly owning one, and being available for it all the time. But then Henri came into my life and I fell in LOVE with him. He was the first thing on my mind, as soon as I flew home, so I immediately went to bring him home. Never having an animal and not really knowing anything about them, my first thought was…*now what the hell do I do?*

Well, Henri is such a huge part of my life, and he has integrated himself into all aspects of my life. He just radiates pure LOVE! Thank you, Henri, for coming into my life.

Chapter Ten

Note To Self

Note To Self

Note To Self

CHAPTER ELEVEN

Bonjour PARIS...Again!

After introducing my friend to my client at the time...and like I have previously stated they're now married. One of the greatest benefits from that new union for me, was that it allowed my friend and I to see each other more often.

She was excited about her new home and life. In one of our many conversations she explained that she really wanted to travel a lot more now, but also realized that her new husband had no interest in traveling. So I suggested that *we should plan a trip ourselves* one day.

When that one day arrived, I just called her up and said, *"Okay...I'm going to Paris on this date-are you in?"* On September of 2006 she, her daughter, and of course me...were off to Paris. I LOVE it there and it's always a plus being able to share a place that you LOVE, with someone else for the first time too.

While we were all sitting on the plane and waiting for it to take off, I kept having the strangest sensation. I even had to say it out loud, *"I don't know what this feeling is* (it's happening again), *but when I get home my life will completely change.*"

When I asked my friend if she remembered us even having that conversation, she had said, "No." But that's okay I have it written in one my journals so I know that I'm not crazy. In fact, I felt it so strongly about it that I think I even said it several times during our trip.

I was very excited about going to Paris. For some reason though, I was also anxiously anticipating the return home, which is so not like me at all. Normally that would be the last thing I would be thinking about. I needed to remind myself that in this moment I was going to Paris, and I'm seeing it again, so that should be the only thing on my mind!

All in all, the trip was great, we all had a good time. But after being back in the states for a couple of weeks, **I had completely forgotten about the intense experience that I had on the plane.** That was until one day when I was driving down the main street of the town that I lived in. As I was approaching this vacant store front, the same store front that I had driven by a million times before, for some reason that day, at that particular moment, it was different. I turned and looked at that store front and I said to myself, *I think I will open a store RIGHT THERE! As I actually pointed at the storefront through my car window.*

For as long as I remember I have always wanted to own my own storefront. I even wondered at times what I would sell, and what would it look like. In fact for many years I even had visions of it possibly being a flower shop, just because I LOVE flowers so much.

I always felt that owning a little flower shop would be so poetically quaint and fun, but not having any experience in that field, and knowing that the inventory has an expiration factor, I pretty much ruled that out quite quickly.

Chapter Eleven

So, with this new found possible store vision and an inner drive building stronger by the day, I sat down and wrote a business plan. It just flowed. I remember doing one much earlier in my life for another business model, and it was like I was pulling teeth. After the plan was all complete, I started reviewing product lines. Then in what felt like days later, had been in fact weeks...I was booking an appointment to go visit the "new" desired store front. Next thing I knew, I was signing the lease. Wow! There it was all coming together...when the time is right...it's just right.

Note To Self

Note To Self

Note To Self

Note To Self

CHAPTER TWELVE

118 W. Main Street Barrington, IL

This is the official address of my very first store, OMG! I could not believe it...I'm a store owner!

Those days of getting ready to open were fast, furious, and very interesting. I had a very limited budget. In fact, I opened the store with so few items, that it truly looked bad. There was nothing on the walls. And I had very little to sell. During those awkward first days of opening, I was constantly thinking, *why didn't I wait a little longer to open so that I could properly gather some more interesting lines?* But, this was my first time out and I was truly flying by the seat of my pants.

I have to say that this first time store owner really didn't make too many mistakes. Money was very limited so I couldn't really afford to make a mistake. Even my lawyer chimed in stating, "You will never make it through year one with such limited funds." Actually, he said the first six months and if I was really lucky, maybe a year!

Needless to say I didn't listen to anyone, and yes I made it through the first year, the second, the third and so on. This just re-establishes my point of needing to only listen to yourself and the importance of finding the strength to remain true to your own visions in life. Because everybody, and I mean everybody, thinks that they have **YOUR** right answers.

The smartest move was, keeping my "open to buy" very conservative. When I opened the store I wanted to see what was moving fast and what was not, so that I could judge what the right direction was for proper buying in my area. I had heard a lot of horror stories of shop owners opening their stores and then just mass merchandising the hell of out of it, all in the name of fear. Fear that they won't have that right thing, at that right time. As life, a shop owner cannot be all things to all people, and still pay your bills.

The major areas to watch when building your own business are inventory and advertising. Do whatever you can for free first. Save the paid advertising campaigns are for the larger establishments. Speaking about the very important aspect of growth, so many have felt in the past if it "plays" well small, can you imagine if we double it not triple the size of the location?

Bigger is not always better; profits don't always double and triple. But your bills do! The most important lesson you should learn is, if you have any desire to open a retail storefront, design your life, then create your business around that. How do you like to spend your time? This is mandatory when setting up shop and determining how you want to run it. Do you like days off? Vacations? Do you like people? Do you like working nights?

Don't be obsessed with being in your store 24/7, in fear that you might miss a client. Never let your business control your life. Have the hours that allow you to run a business properly of course, but have a life too. Whether that means you need a staff or just limited hours. The most important thing to remember, is to make sure that your business allows you to feel that you're still connected to your life, and that your business is not running you.

When I opened my store I found out how true, the old adage is, *that everything happens for a reason.* Having such a varied background helped me get from me from point "a" to point "b" while feeling very comfortable at taking on all the tasks of creating that entire endeavor myself.

Everything from the designing, displaying, and of course all of the buying. I feel that you have to have the most important aspect of all, and that is the desire for great customer service. Because it's how you treat your clients/customers that will build your business. Everything…and I mean everything I learned throughout my life helped me to cultivate my business brand.

…*Welcome!*

My store had been open for several months and things were really starting to fall into place. I was feeling so much more comfortable about which direction to go into for ordering product. The business was picking up month after month. It was really quite exciting watching it grow!

One day, sitting in the store I realized that I still, really didn't have that much on the walls. I thought…what I'm I doing? I have all of my own art work at home, so one day I decided to bring a large portion of that art to the store/studio.

I have had my art in a gallery before, but I had to pull it out. It just didn't feel like that particular gallery owner was the right fit for me. Plus, the gallery owner didn't seem to value my work and I felt that it was reflected in the pricing she had placed on my art, so I removed them.

Before I hung my art in the store, I didn't even think twice of how the public could have responded to the actual pieces. I was completely oblivious to the opinions that I could have been subjected to. But after a short time of hearing what people had said about my art, it was really quite shocking to me. They said a lot of the same things that I wanted to convey when I was actually creating the work. In fact, 95% of all of the comments were very complimentary.

How wonderful it was that something that started out as an element to just fill up my wall space, was becoming a personal and financial success. I LOVE happy coincidences…serendipity strikes again!

I was well into my second year when the recession of 2008 took hold of the nation. Even though I truly felt that there was a protective bubble over our that area. Being that it's a very affluent town, the effects weren't felt quite as strongly on a local standpoint…yet. Even though my numbers were pretty good for being a new shop owner, I was still buying into a lot of the head games of fear of the attachment. I was constantly trying not to entertain the possibility of losing what I dreamed about having for so long.

If you can remember back a few chapters, when I was writing about my experience of packing up everything and moving to California, and that I didn't really not having any issues with fear at all in my choice to move out of state. Nor did I feel that the word "fear" was even

Chapter Twelve

in my vocabulary. I also stated that one day I might find out just how untrue that last statement would be for me. Well, the experience of opening up my store, and having thoughts of losing my dream, brought my own personal day of reckoning and tipping point.

With the combination of a bad economy and being so new at this business. I soon realized that everyone can be subjected to fear at one time or another in their life. What I really discovered, was that fear hits hard with your depth of ATTACHMENT. Especially when that need is attached to a specific desired outcome, then that overrides everything. It then makes you dependent on that "element" which can be anything from a person, place to a thing. That's what we really need to be aware of in life. To never allow yourself to form an emotional dependence on anything or anyone.

When manifesting dreams and desires you must be able to totally let go of any wanted outcome. That of course became my own personal struggle at that time with the store. This philosophy can be very easily stated, but it can be very difficult to apply, unfortunately. Truly embracing this philosophy, is where true peace lays.

Though I can totally understand this philosophy and rally to try to apply it now, the store, was a daily struggle. When I first opened my shop the mere thought of not having it, drove me deep into the depths of fear. So much so, that my hair began to fall out from the stress. OMG...my hair! That's huge for a girl. Who wants to look at a bald, stressed out shop owner? But I worked on my health, tried to relax and I through time it all grew back...thank goodness!

Lesson Learned: *Fear is an illusion that we all buy into at one point or another in our lives. The goal when we're caught in the nets of "fear" is to stop struggling. Let go, and release whatever we think we MUST be doing. Try to remember to be unattached to the desired outcome. It just might even bring you more positive avenues than you ever dreamed of.*

Chapter Twelve

Note To Self

Note To Self

Note To Self

CHAPTER THIRTEEN

New Store Location?

It was September of 2008 and I was nearing the end of my lease at 118 W. Main. I had only signed on for a couple of years for my first time out. Once again I found myself at a difficult crossroads. Do I stay here on Main Street or do I move to a new location? I needed answers. As far as my very definitive decision making skills go, those were greatly tested once again because of the amount of my emotional attachment. It's frustrating being at the crossroads of trying to decide on which avenue will have the best outcome. We have all been there at one time or another. Thinking, does this particular choice or direction make it better or worse?

So, like any good decision maker, I decided to stop over-thinking. I stopped trying to kill myself over this need to choose, and I tried to let it go. Then one day while I was working in the shop, I kept noticing something. It seemed like every other customer (*an over exaggeration*), but at least one customer every other day, for about a couple of weeks. Where someone would walk into my shop and say, "Wow you know what this place reminds me of...it reminds me of Carmel!" I would reply, "*Carmel, California?*" They usually respond with a yes. I of course would be so taken back by the correlation, and of course thank them for the lovely compliment.

Then I had this epiphany, that maybe this was another sign. Okay, I know what you're thinking, but they laughed at Edison too, so whatever works, go with it...I always say!

Remember when I was trying to decide if I should stay, or go back home when I was living in Carmel? I decided to listen to my gut and follow the universal direction.

So, I decided to go for it!

The next day I called the landlord, and I told him that I would not be renewing my lease. I went on to explain that I would be moving to a new location and when I hung up the phone I then realized it was the right choice all along. Is that *déjà vu* that I'm feeling?

...it started with just a picture!

When I was first thinking about having a storefront. I had always wanted to have a flower shop. Though I'm very aware of the fact that the inventory needs to move out on a daily basis otherwise you will lose money, so that pretty much ruled out those desires right away for me. But that LOVE for flowers never rested.

Being a designer, I had numerous clients that would request an alternative to silks for their homes. They just couldn't stand the look of fake flowers, and I couldn't have agreed with them more.

So, one day I went through some magazines, which was one of my biggest indulgences before Pinterest, and I came across this picture of a room. There was nothing extraordinary about the room, it just had the most simple and clean arrangements in it. They just seem to jump right off the page.

As soon as I saw them, I was so inspired to create something similar. And as much as I love big beautiful REAL green plants, I didn't want the maintenance of real plants.

I became obsessed in recreating the plants that were in this picture. So I researched the hell out of the internet, desperately searching for an alternative. I could not believe it, I found something online! These greens were from a farm in North Carolina. I ordered them right away, and as soon as they arrived I of course assembled them into an arrangement.

Chapter Thirteen

These botanicals which I called "greens," seemed to be that perfect solution. These plants were systemically sealed in their natural state. More importantly they're real and they never need maintenance. In fact, I even still use them in my home today. So, after making a couple arrangements, and watching them fly off the shelves. I felt that I had found the keys to the kingdom of a possible niche. It would be safe to say that those "greens" literally took over my business.

It's so weird how things happen and how they manifest. Sometimes from a simple photograph, a vision, or just something nagging at your intuition. I believe that your intuition is your life's messenger. Knocking, and giving you a hints and a direction. These "new" directions don't always come with the parting of the seas or a burning bush. They come softly. That's why your mind needs to be still to hear your heart's desire. It's then your job to decide if you want to follow through or not. Life is always about choice.

Lesson Learned: *The Law of Attraction has been so over marketed that I feel it has lost its true essence. What many don't realize is that there are many universal laws. But this particular one, has been bastardized to no end. Many feel that once they put a wish out there that it should materialize in a matter of days. To me, that's NOT the law of attraction. LOA-is simply having a vision and then allowing that energy into your life. By letting go of all expectations of a desired outcome. Putting the desire out to the universe and then having the patience to see how and when it comes back to you.*

Note To Self

Note To Self

Note To Self

CHAPTER FOURTEEN

Is That You?

Moving the business to a brand new mall created just outside of town was very exciting. I just never realized how exciting it would actually get. Until the day that David decided to walk through my front door…20 years after we said good-bye.

I usually don't work on Sunday's, but this particular week the person that usually covers the store was not able to work. As I would soon find out that, that particular day would not turn out to be just like any other ordinary day. I had just finished all my usual start of the day procedures when I was opening some email. One particular email got my attention right away. It was a Facebook contact, asking me if I was the same person that he had known along time ago.

It was August 2009, and I could not believe my eyes. It was David. After all this time. I could barely hold back my excitement. I needed to respond right away. In fact, I never even thought twice. My hands were shaking as I placed my fingers on the keyboard. What do I say? I had so much that I would LOVE to ask, but I also want to hold back. Typical Gail!

After composing the letter and then hitting send, I had a very difficult time waiting for him to respond back. But his email finally arrived. I was so excited to hear from him again, after so many years. I truly felt it was the aphrodisiac that my soul truly hungered for.

After a couple of exchanges back and forth. I finally asked him the big question, "A*re you still married?*" Of course, I buffered it with other filler questions, but that was the only question I wanted an answer to. His response came the next day. I sped through the letter to find the only real answer I was truly searching for, "YES, I'm still married!"

My heart dropped. I don't know what I was thinking or even why I was so disappointed. But I was. You might think that I wanted the answer to be no, hoping that he had come back into my life to claim my heart again. That's not actually true.

So much time had passed and being in other relationships widened my expectations. **I don't know if David would be the one again. Especially after all of this time.** But after a couple of emails were exchanged back in forth, I felt that their really was no reason to keep writing, so I just stopped.

Then about a month after I stopped writing, he just walked right through the front door of my shop. Interesting how he knew where it was.

The first thing I said was, "David, David is that you?"

His response, "I know...I got old." I couldn't believe my eyes. At first, I didn't recognize him. His body, his height, was the same as I remembered, but his face, it was different.

He cut off his beautiful hair. Why? He had such long thick hair. It was just all buzzed off. Had age taken something from him...like it eventually does to us all? I don't know exactly what it was, but something was different. That was just the physical.

Speaking of physical, I looked horrible. If I'd known he was coming I would have at least worn makeup. OMG...seriously!

At first, it was really awkward, but I eventually got over how bad I looked. Then we really started talking about old times. No matter what this whole chance encounter was about, I just wanted him to remember me in a good way. I did enjoy the fact that he was clearly nervous. I felt, that him taking the time to come and find me showed that this was something very important to him too, back then.

He had obvious signs of being nervous. He kept asking for water and he was sweating a lot. After an hour or two of just small talk, he left. It took awhile for the initial shock to wear off and really embrace how great it was in seeing him again. In fact, I think that it might have been too good seeing him.

Later after David left, one of the neighboring store owners came over to tell me that he noticed the guy that just left my store, sitting in his car. *"I think he was out there for about half hour before he got the courage to come in."* He also stated, *that he kept looking in the mirror and fixing his hair-he seemed very nervous.*

It was great to hear that maybe David was just as nervous as I was.

After his visit, he called a couple of times, I couldn't help but feel that I had been really quite cold to David. Perhaps I had my walls up. Perhaps??? Walls up? Girl please, a hook and ladder truck couldn't have scaled the walls that I had up.

A few months later David called again, saying that he would be coming by my area, wondering if he could stop by. I was pretty stoked that I would have another opportunity to see him. Especially since the previous time I really hadn't been prepared. I wanted him to remember me looking a lot better than I did the last time he saw him. I, of course, was thinking how short can you wear a dress, before it starts looking like a shirt?

...make-up, better outfit, check!

Our meeting was a little more comfortable the second time around. Perhaps it was because I felt I looked a lot better. Or maybe it was because we had such a strong connection. Either way, I enjoyed the fact that our connection was still there, but my guarded demeanor was slowly snuck back in. In fact within a short time it became quite evident. Yes, I really enjoyed seeing him again I just wanted more, I wanted him to throw his arms around me and tell me that he had missed me.

We talked for quite awhile exchanging stories from the past. In those stories I told him about two women that had walked into my old shop in the village.

The incident that I was referring to, happened at one of my side-walk sale days. These two women had been in my store and I noticed that they were speaking Serbian. I had not heard that language in a while, but I recognized it immediately. I asked them where they were from. They told me. Then I went on to explain that someone that I knew a long time ago, was from Serbia; hearing them speak reminded me of that time.

Then one of the ladies asked me what his name was. Normally I don't share his complete name, but that time I did. Unbelievably her reply was, "That's my husband's best friend.

They have been best friends for a long time. But unfortunately, they no longer speak."

I couldn't believe it. What are the odds?

We talked for awhile and as she was told me a little about David, I asked her some simple questions, hopefully trying not to appear to eager…but I was. In fact, I was screaming inside…OMG…OMG!

I couldn't let it show. In case they once again crossed paths with David. So, after we exchanged all the basic niceties, they went on their way. For just a moment I

Chapter Fourteen

was teleported from my shop of everyday, to the most incredible essence of bliss, reliving that LOVING energy that I had once had for someone so special.

Small little coincidences or name associations seemed to escalate with time after that. Magnetizing with time, and it just got surreal. Were all these situations coincidence, or was a higher vibration aligning itself? Who would ever have known that a year after this chance encounter with these ladies. David would actually walk into my store? Without him ever knowing about how I met some friends of his just a short time back.

On New Years 2010, my caller ID to told me that David tried calling. He never left a message. Months went by, and I'm afraid that he was still on my mind. Then one day I decided to email him, asking to see him. I needed to explain that if I appeared like I wasn't comfortable or distant, it was because of my defensiveness or should I say my need to protect my heart. The email explained that I was unsure of his original intentions, and that I would like to talk to him. I had felt so badly about how I handled myself. Even my sister felt that I was so stand-offish to someone that meant so much to me.

WE didn't see each other again until May 2010, two months after I sent that email. The energy just flowed. We sat and had a drink at a little Parisian place (how perfect). I did most of the talking, telling him how I felt the last time we saw each other, that I was really holding back. He said that he had noticed. I explained, that what he did took a lot of courage, and I really admire that type of courage. David taking the time to seek me out, really made me feel special and I will always have that. I told him all about my life now and how it has changed, that I did not blame him for the break-up, and that I was not mad. Even though I probably couldn't have said that for at least two years after we broke up. Kidding. I was more numb than mad back then.

Looking back it was all meant to be. We sat there sharing how our lives had progressed. I was so excited to hear that he had children, a boy and a girl.

While reminiscing about our past, I was also noticed something about the way he was responded to certain aspects of our conversation. It was his expression, as though I was telling him something for the first time. Like he was not connecting the dots, with some of the memories.

Well, he finally told me that he had a memory lapses. That a lot of his childhood memories and things that happened in his earlier years were just lost. He really had no explanation for it. I could not help but think of one particular time that may have been a probable cause for his memory loss: the horrible car accident that had happened while we were still together.

When I was updating a friend of mine about this whole David situation, him coming into the store, she found it so ironic about his memory loss. If I look at it from the holistic standpoint, the issue of his loss of memory, it may have been a way for him to cope with a loss of a great LOVE. I would like to think that's true

Chapter Fourteen

too, but one will never really know.

The night of the accident, was another one of those markers in life where everything stops, and it's forever etched in time.

It was about a year or so before we had actually broken up. A phone call came into the house just after midnight. There was a man on the other end of phone line asking if I was David's wife. I said, "No *I'm not his wife.*" This person went on to say, "That's strange because David gave me this phone number and asked me to call his wife. To let her know that he had been a serious car accident."

I'm afraid that my response was not very good. In fact, I'm a little embarrassed to admit that I got quite upset. I said, " *I don't know who this is, but you have the wrong number. I'm not married!*" I just hung up the phone and went back to sleep. I didn't even try to call David to see if he would pick up the phone. Not my finest hour.

The next day I found out that it was all true…he had been in a very serious accident.

After he told me of his memory loss I wondered if that car accident had any correlation. I was extremely shocked, but it would make sense. So, then I needed to ask him the big question. "*Do you remember asking to marry me?*" My heart broke…he said no!

It wasn't that the proposal had been something very special. In fact, it was just the opposite. I wanted to be with him, he wanted that too…at that time. We were in the kitchen kissing and doing what couples do. He said we should be together and possibly get married. I said, "Then let's live together first, and then in time get engaged." No big major event just two people wanting the same thing, to be together. So I thought.

I think of all that has happened between him and I, David, taking the time to contact me again and making me feel so very special, it was such a gift. Many times I have had fun fantasizing of what could have happened, but I point-blank asked him what his intentions were in contacting me again after all these years. I stated that, *"I would never be interested in an affair."* He replied that, "He wouldn't be either, and that he couldn't do that to his wife." I'm also very much aware that when David was young his parents had divorced, and I know how deeply he had been affected by that.

Many of you may judge him negatively for even showing up at my door to begin with. But it was the reverse for me, I had even more respect for him after he stated his dedication to his family. I want to believe that his obligation to his family was much more important than fulfilling anything temporary.

When we broke up all those years ago, I remember I purposely never said the words...good-bye. This time when we saw each other in May of 2010. I knew that I had to say the words, GOOD-BYE.

We were sitting in my car after having a couple of drinks at the cafe. You could cut the energy with a knife it was so thick, I needed to get out of that car

Chapter Fourteen

quick because I could have just reached over and kissed him. It was so intense the energy between us. Instead, I stuck my hand out for us to shake. It was contact, an ability to touch him, but a respectable one. Our hands remained clasped as we exchanged our final words.

I said, *"That our energy is like water-it just flows and that if we're not to be together in this life time. Maybe we will be together in our next lifetime."* I then let go of his hand and it took everything that I had to get out of the car. As David got out of the driver's seat of my car, he held my car door open, as I got into the driver's seat. He was about to close the door and then I said the words… GOOD-BYE David. The words I had always dreaded. With that, the door was shut, and I just drove off.

Driving home, such a peaceful feeling came over me. Two glasses of wine also helped with that. As I was pulling into the driveway my cell phone rang. It was David. I used to always judge a man's interest in me after a date, by how soon he called me again. Even though this was not a date, I still found it very interesting and so endearing, his need to have contact with me again so soon after.

He said, "I wanted to show you something, something that I forgot about, so I will just have to wait until another time." *I said, "Yes David another time."* There was a sound of subtle excitement in his voice, those tones that are only used when talking to someone you have a great deal of attraction too. I enjoyed hearing it in his voice. It made me feel good. That sense of familiarity came rushing over me again. But I knew that there would *not* be another time. Unless something changed in his life. This sense of knowing…a knowing of what you want and most importantly what you don't want in life. Most importantly, the comfort to express it. It was fabulously fulfilling. It's an essence of complete contentment. That cannot be bottled.

But what was this knowing? Was it about knowing that I had LOVED and lost, and that LOVE would find me again? Or was it that he truly did LOVE me and that he never forgot about me? One memory that I will hold tight to was when we were saying goodbye. As we hugged, his words, the mere sound of his voice, saying the words, "This feels so good." I was thinking yes, yes it does. Secretly wishing…how I could I only have more of *this*.

I spent many years pursuing dreams in my life, mainly desiring to create a name for myself. My misunderstanding of life might be my legacy, during that quest to become a self-made woman. My vision in life has changed now. Maybe, I wasn't here to capture some elusive dream. Perhaps something far simpler. Maybe, I was just capable of great LOVE.

David called once again…I never picked up the phone it went to voice mail. It was one of the rare times that he had left a message; it took me months to delete it.

Chapter Fourteen

Note To Self

Note To Self

Note To Self

CHAPTER FIFTEEN

How Many Times Does One Need to Say Goodbye in a Lifetime?

It's Friday, and it's Valentine's Day weekend 2011. I'm at the store and just getting back from walking Henri. The phone is ringing as I walk in the store. As I reach for the phone I notice that the caller ID's last three letters read ICH. Could this be him? It is!

It's always so good to hear his voice and I told him that. We exchanged small talk, then he said that he would like to see me. At first, *I said, "NO."* I explained, *"David it's really hard for me when I see you, it really stirs up a lot of old emotions."* He insisted, so I asked for some time to think about it. Well, that lasted about five days and then emailed him back stating that I had come to a decision and to please call me for the answer.

The call came about half hour after I sent the email. David stated that he would be going away for the next couple of weekends and that he would call me back when he had a better idea of when we could possibly get together. He made some reference to time, like we have plenty of time now. English is not his first language, so I need to always take that into account. I stated, *"I understand and at the time when you do call, we will have to see if both of our schedules will work to get together."* With that, we hung up.

We weren't able to get together until March 12, 2011. I was in Chicago all day with a client, and he arrived at my store around 5:30. It had been almost a year since I had seen him. He always looks good to me. Even though his hair was so damn short! His energy and vibration is just so right. We just "click". How does this attraction still stay so strong…though we are not together? Why is it not dissipating with time?

You know what is so amazing, I'm sure that there are a lot of women who can really relate to this. Those laundry lists that we keep in our heads? You know the ones that say, tall, handsome, funny….blah, blah, blah. It's amazing how all that goes out the window when the connection is just there.

Now back to reality. We went out for dinner and everything was great. It always is. I said it before and I will say it again…it just flows. Well, my objective was to understand what we were doing. So, I tried to find just the right time. Should it be at the beginning, middle… whatever? Finally, I just said it, *"David, what are we doing here?"* Long pause then David stated, "Well, I wanted to see you. I had such a great time the last time we got together, I wanted to see you again."

I tried to understand and stay patient with his evasiveness, but I got no answers. I needed to understand. I wished that it could be that simple and that we could be friends, so that we could call each other when we want to just talk about things that are going on in our own individual lives. Unfortunately, time did not remove the incredibly deep sexual chemistry that I have for him. Not a good combination for me. Obviously, he was still married.

I began to explain my position he refused to discuss his. *"You had taken a vow a long time ago and with that vow, I would think that would include you giving up seeing other women." Is* that a little tone I hear in my voice...YES. I went on to say, "Or *let me at least preface that by saying... at least this particular woman is not interested in seeing you while your married."*

"I don't know how many other women you have called up from your past and asked to see, but I'm afraid I DO NOT see married men...period. The only reason why I'm sitting here today, is that you once represented something very special in my life. When we saw each other last year in May. I said, goodbye."

The expression on David's face dropped and appeared drained of emotion. Great, now I have pushed it too far? Then David just said, "That's not how I heard it. Maybe I need to listen better." *Gee...do you think?* As soon as he stopped talking the energy immediately shifted. So much so that it was palatable. In fact, I even said, "W*ow, did you feel that?* David said, "Yes." Now, how obvious is

Chapter Fifteen

that…that even he could feel the energy shift.

I quickly asked him some other questions and the energy went back up. In fact, I was feeling so comfortable that I even approached it from another angle, but he was pretty set that there was no specific reason. As I tried to let it go, he turned the tables on me, asking me, "Then why are their large question marks in your eyes?"

My reply was, *"Are there question marks in my eyes? Maybe you can answer them for me?"* David said, "We're right back here again." Excuse me, can someone please remove the "dead horse" from table 8…please! Thank you!

We finished our meal, and made our way out to the parking lot. David tried to hug me, but I pushed away. Little does he know that's all I wanted him to do, but it wasn't appropriate at all.

The next thing I knew, we were back in front of my store and I was trying to quickly exit. Exit everything, but mainly the awkwardness of that moment. I stated that I needed to go in and close down the shop for the day. David asked if he could come in and use the washroom. I of course said, "Yes." Part of me didn't want him to, but the other part really did. Are you still with me here? Yes, I want my cake and eat it too…and that cake is David!

David sat on one of the counters as I finished shutting down the store. He asked if he could smoke a cigar, and boy he looked damn sexy doing it too, and I can't stand cigars. OMG!

We talked for about an hour, but I really needed to leave. As we both walk out together, I stopped to lock the door. I wanted to make a mad run for my car, and drive as fast as I could away from there, leaving him standing there with no clue of what just happen. I was just plain sick and tired of always "saying good-bye" to this man.

We walked towards my car. David opened my car door. As I tried to get in the driver's seat. David reached in to attempt to give me a hug...but I was a stone. Then he said, "Well since you said that this is difficult for you, have a good life."

"OK...David...you too." Is that more tone I hear in my voice? Yes! Can somebody please throw me a life ring! David continued, "If you ever get the book published, please promise to send me a copy." I said that I would, then he said, "You never know maybe our path's will cross again." With that I said, *"You never know."* And *I* pulled away.

For days I re-lived those last moments, but you cannot change what is. So I decided to email him this note:

I needed you to know that I felt that Friday night's ending was a little rough. It was all I could do to leave and keep my morals intact. This has been a wonderful experience seeing you again. But like I stated to you on the phone when you asked to see me...it's way too difficult. We share a strong connection. You know what holds me back...so if that was to ever change... and you grow your hair out (LOL)...you will know where to find me. Because you will always have a place in my heart.

Chapter Fifteen

AML-G

I felt so much better after I sent that out to David. Almost as though you can feel the Karma complete itself.

Note To Self

Note To Self

Note To Self

Note To Self

CHAPTER SIXTEEN

The Journey Still Continues as I... Surrender to LOVE

Seeing David several times since those first moments back in 2009, was both euphoric and torturous all in the same breath. Euphoric for obvious reasons and torturous from the standpoint of everytime I laid eyes on him, I was reminded of what I want, but still seek. Not so much the person, David. Because I really don't know who he is any longer. More the essence or feeling that I have in his presence. That's what I seek again. That sense of peace and knowing that you get when you're in the presence of a great LOVE. That's the LOVE that I am seeking, and especially to have reflected back to me. My fear (and yes...I know that fear is not "surrendering", but I'm being real here) is...can I recapture that again with someone else?

My path of never settling for anything less in life then the complete LOVE that I seek. Because that's what I truly feel I deserve. Someone that reflects back to me that much needed 100% comfort and acceptance in their presence.

That also carries over in my personal and professional relationships. My comfort is the priority. I know what I want, and what I don't want. This type of knowing, perhaps even bordering on stubbornness can be very difficult to relate to. I completely understand that, but I also wish others would have more of a appreciation of what they feel they deserve. To be more discerning, than to allow anything but complete love, kindness, and support through all of their connections. I have seen so many settle for what they felt "their" expectations of LOVE was, versus what it COULD really be.

A connection so deep, that when you're looking into our LOVEs eyes, it's as though you're seeing into their soul. When you're holding a gaze with someone special, and it comes with a feeling that you are the only two, all alone in a crowded room, and time virtually stands still. That's what I crave for again.

I have experienced it once, and it was still there. At least for me. That day, when he walked through my door, he brought that energy back into my life. That LOVE energy. The LOVE energy that's real and everlasting, especially when it is pure and uncaptured.

I feel that when we enter marriages those boundaries are sacrosanct. The boundaries in marriage are like stating to the world I LOVE YOU. I choose you. I bestow unto you the name, "my husband" and I, "your wife." And with that vow, I then trust that you will cherish and take care of my heart.

Once that LOVE is no longer mutual and freely shared between us, that is when we need to come to together to release what we once knew as a shared connection and a place of safety. So, that we can now be free to find another.

This idea of a connection or marriage, I think is what so many have a problem with. They want to possess this LOVE (the other person) that they found...forever! Through that need...comes a desire for control. Then that need becomes a demand. You better LOVE me...I have devoted so many years to this relationship. But you cannot demand LOVE...it must come freely.

Obviously divorce happens all the time. What most people don't seem to understand is how they got there. That path is usually paved with a long road of how they wanted LOVE. How they withheld LOVE. And how they forgot to LOVE, because life got to busy or too mundane. Some simply, just stop trying to connect.

Sometimes this losing of LOVE, simply might be that you have come to the end of your relationship. What? There are expiration dates on LOVE? In away...yes! Your desires and aspirations in life change all the time. And of course people change too. So, unless you're both are very connected to your own growth and growth as a couple, things might be forced to change. You can still feel LOVE for someone, but no longer desire to be married to that person. When your soul is hungry for change...it occurs sooner or later.

When involved in a marriage for years, it's difficult to

desire change. The routine is there and fear comes with change. Fear of what will happen to all of the relationships that are involved within that union. Children, in-laws, that, can be very scary. But if your bleeding unhappiness maybe it's time to hit the review or the reset button. The marriage doesn't have to end for change to occur. Maybe it's just time to reassess each other's desires in life, and reconnect with a new perspective.

But living under the same roof and not expressing LOVE, or admiration for each other can be detrimental. When you start forgetting how to care about the other person's feelings, that is just selfish, and it shows that you're just checking out of the marriage or relationship, and what life has to offer in that shared connection.

I can't even imagine how torturous this type of relationship must be. To co-exist under the same roof with someone that you had once chosen out of LOVE. Now there basically just filling a role, Wife, Husband, Mother or Father. A role that you have been living for years, and now it's just become complacent. Time, has brought distance between you both. It's as though you're like roommates. Keeping a fair distance away, just so that you don't have to deal with each other's intimacy issues.

As I have said before...I'm fascinated by the dynamics of LOVE. What brings people together in the first place? Where does LOVE go when divorce occurs? How come that same relationship which once was so filled with LOVE, years later can turn into bitterness, anger or complacency?

Why is it that we hide our true feelings from each other? Why is it that those who say that they're in LOVE choose to knowingly hurt the other…to make themselves feel better? Why do couples need to have control over the other in order to feel that they are being heard or taken care of? In other words, demanding LOVE out of fear that it won't be given freely *(look at everything I do for you)*?

Are we all destined to meet that one (possibly two) true LOVE's, soulmates, or twin flames in a lifetime? And my favorite question of all…what makes a man or a woman unforgettable?

If you have been fortunate enough to find that someone special. That person who is your everything. Someone that you totally trust with all of your heart to be there, to support you emotionally and spiritually, who only seeks to find your strengths and not your weaknesses, then you're truly blessed!

There are countless philosophies, stories, advice and even directions for how LOVE can be defined and obtained. So much so, that book stores fill huge sections of their shelves on this elusive topic alone. Do I personally feel that there is one perfect formula? No! What I do know and I have said it several times during this book, is that we must all **BELIEVE, SURRENDER, LOVE.**

Believing is seeing. Seeing what can come into your

life. Surrender to the concepts of why it's not playing out the way we thought it would. And finally just being LOVE. By being patient, being kind and most of all being compassionate and understanding to all. Even those that set out to hurt you.

We sometimes allow ourselves and others to be treated in ways that are not always acceptable. Some may even have done things to manipulate another person or situation in order to obtain something. Perhaps, even throwing away or undermining their own individual core values and needs, all for some attention. That's what I would like to see change. For us to stop undervaluing our own inner beauty and intelligence.

...there's only one you, so be it!

Everyone has moments when they question one element or another in their life. From their weight, dress, career, perhaps even family issues. **There will always be something that temporarily rocks our inner strength. But that doesn't mean that you should** ever let a man or women disrespect or offer you less than you deserve. Never ever…no matter who they are.

When you understand this very important fact, and put yourself first, more importantly putting your feelings first. Not demanding, or whining to get your way in life with others. But explaining what you need in life to feel LOVED, embraced and safe. There is something spectacular about a woman who owns that inner confidence, it's sexy. It has nothing to do with dressing completely obvious-that is typical. She is about being very comfortable in her own knowledge of what she wants and doesn't want in her life and has very little patience for "BS." Being typical is for everyone else. Being unforgettable is about being unique and not doing what is expected.

This is not a generational thing...it's a woman's thing. No matter what age or what decade you're reading this book, this book is about knowing what your dreams are in life, having an opinion, and having a strong personal sense of strength. More importantly it's about ot being afraid to be vulnerable, while persevering through all obstacles in life.

Never be afraid to show your emotions. One of my many favorite phrases is... *tears are the anti-freeze to your soul. In* 2012, I think I cried more that year alone...than I did in my entire life (which by the way had nothing to do with or about a man).

I cried for the disappointments and all of the judgment and pain that was projected on me. I couldn't understand those who tried to change me to their ideal of the world. Most of all I cried while a chapter of my life was coming to a close. Possibly all of that emotion was from being vulnerable and scared of what was to come.

I'm just sorry that some needed to kick me even more, when I was down. Perhaps they did because of their own fears. Their need to question my strength and integrity. Their inability to process how I could have

Chapter Sixteen

shown such weakness. Especially when I have carried myself with such strength previously.

I have chosen forgiveness, but most importantly forgiveness for myself. I chose to show this by moving forward without them. If you couldn't cherish the gift of our friendship, then I must move forward without you.

Never be taken down by mere words of others, for they are more broken then you. There is only ONE you…so be it!

Life is not about being strong at the weakness of others. Life is where we all feel very vulnerable, and do not like to surrender to the moment. Through vulnerability and surrendering comes empowerment…not power over another.

Gail J. Kueker

Note To Self

Note To Self

Note To Self

Note To Self

CHAPTER SEVENTEEN

The Audacity of Moving Forward!

The lure of life and its mysteries that surround me is what propels me forward.
Gail J. Kueker

I have one particular childhood memory that comes to mind every so often. It was a time with my Grandmother, and we were in the kitchen of my childhood home. I was probably about 9 or 10. I really can't remember my exact age. But as we were standing there in the kitchen, she was holding my hands and looking at them very closely.

For some reason she was really taken back by them. She was looking at them, turning them over...examining them so close. It almost seemed like she was making sure nothing was wrong with them. While holding them, she had shared this with me...and I'm roughly quoting her because it has been a few years. *"These hands will do good things one day!"* My first thought was, what a strange thing to say. Is that all you got to say... my hands??? You're my Grandmother, aren't you supposed to be gushing over me and pinching my cheeks and telling me how pretty I am.

As I sit here and type these words I now understand how profound her insight was, so long ago. My whole life and everything that I feel that I have done up to now to express my soul's music…was obviously using my hands. As a child I had no inkling that someday I would spend my life painting, designing and creating. So Grandma Krueger, as one artist to another, I now understand. And from what Mom has shared about you Grandma, it seems that we both would have had many similar desires in life. I wish that we could have sat and talked about our mutual creative visions and desires.

Needless to say…with my hands in tow I have set out my entire life creating, building, and achieving. All while trying to **express** my deepest desires in life. And with that said, though my path was a chosen one and at times it brought me limitations. I have always been very happy in my pursuits.

Now looking back I never thought that my true obstacle in life would be people. Even as a child I always made friends very easy. In fact, I can even remember moments of extreme arrogance, of choosing not to be friends with some people that wanted to be friends with me.

But the older I get, the more particular I have become. Not from a selfish perspective, more like a tolerance level. I just have very little patience for those who choose to be narcissistic, self-involved, and angry. I truly desire to connect with people with the same sense of purpose. Those with an ability to understand, a desire for a mutual dialog, not a monologue. And of course, those who are open, emphatic, and have compassion towards others.

It's like when you're in high school, and everybody wants to know, and be like the popular girl or guy. Looking to possess those qualities that others deem acceptable. But at that age your true essence really hasn't had an opportunity to find its own comfort zone. You really have no idea of what your true desires are in life... yet. So, at that age you're out there searching for people to emulate. Then as we get older, it's all about where we live and what we have. Feeling validated once again through acceptance of others.

This searching is difficult. We're trying to find the right "fit" in our lives. Our desires should be about what makes YOU happy. Life is NOT about living up to the expectations of others. That is emotional immaturity. Stay open, stay positive and grow with your life experiences. Always look to be involved with those who are more...**EVOLVED** in life.

It's still shocking to me to see the depths emotional immaturity. On how far some will go to hurt and manipulate others for their own personal gain and satisfaction. I have enjoyed the experience of meeting many new people and getting really close with a select few. Though it always shocks me, when women actually choose to be personally and professionally cruel to other women. Even worse yet, obtaining a deep sense of satisfaction from it.

Chapter Seventeen

Life is about finding balance. Balance of extremes in our daily interactions. When you're able to put your ego aside. And observe others. Observe and not react to their need for drama. That's when you're "winning."

Please never allow others to undermine you or side track you from your visions in life. If there is only one primary message that you take from this book/journal. Please let it be the fact that your journey in life is about **SELF-ACCEPTANCE,** not about self-improvement.

It took me so long to get this. Before I truly started to embrace this very important aspect of life, I always felt that it was as though I was always missing something or some part of the "magic" formula. And if I just had that magic formula, it could unlock all of the doors.

That was until I realized that the magic formula is about your own acceptance and desire for self-empowerment, not improvement.

This doesn't mean that if you broke your nose a couple of times, that you should just accept the fact that you have a crooked nose, and can't breathe right. No! Get it corrected. The acceptance and empowerment is about knowing that what you offer in life, is enough!

Yes...we all like to "gild the lily," I believe that is the old phrase? But, when you don't like or accept yourself for who you are as a person in general, no amount of cosmetic changes will help.

It's all about knowing your strengths as well as your weaknesses. Until you adopt this philosophy of complete self-acceptance, I feel that you will always be searching for LOVE and happiness *through others and material aspects.*

...acceptance to persevere is the definition of success!

I have often heard how other people define success in life. Some see success as your profession, to the possessions that we purchase. **To me, success is the ability to find the courage to persevere in life. Seeing your visions (dreams) come to fruition no matter the obstacles.**

Those that just sit on the sidelines of life wanting "to do" things, but never have the courage to even start, or worse yet, enjoy critiquing others that do try-I feel that those are the true definition of fear and failure.

Oprah's definition of success and in her opinion success is, "Women supporting women. In other words, when you help empower and strengthen other women. Helping them raise up, instead of sabotaging others or by being purposely mean to them." **Amen girlfriend!**

I have personally witnessed this, women hurting other women, all because they feel threatened by their strength, their beauty. Even their mere presence would be enough to make some feel less.

This book is a great example of persevering through other peoples perception's. My 4th grade English teacher shared with me one day in between classes. *"That I could barely even put two sentences together to save my life."*

Chapter Seventeen

Perhaps he was right. All I know is that...I will always try. And for all you armchair critiques reading this and possibly agreeing with him, you can just put this book down now...and go find one of those projects that you always say you're going to start or finish. Because my intention was to complete my thoughts and feelings on paper, not create the next best-selling novel.

But that's just it...through almost every major project or milestone I have dreamed of. I had to overcome some type of adversity. Whether it was someone advising me not to try, limited finances or my own self-doubt. Many will protest reasons why it should never be done. And there might even be some that will just flat out say, "It can't be done." **It's your job to believe in yourself and persevere.**

I feel that many people would LOVE to experience creating something from the ground up, so that they too, can feel the pride of accomplishment of seeing their projects come to life. But many never actually start...let alone even complete those projects.

This is why so many will ridicule, dismiss, and even find fault with those who do prevail through all obstacles to complete their visions. If you want to see someone who lives in fear, watch the ones that turn on you when things are good, or worse yet when things go bad. They will be the first ones to say, "I told you so." Those are the ones that live with the regret at the end of their life.

...life always brings you new opportunities!

Being a free and happy soul has been my own personal mantra for years. But that was greatly tested in 2012. It was shortly after the start of 2012, the start of my 6th year in business when **I decided to close my store.**

I had hoped at that time when I was closing the store, that maybe I would someday down the road, re-open the store again. Back in the village where I had originally started. A place so small that you could barely turn-around in it. Just a place to call my own again. Where I could make some arrangements and nothing else. But because of the multitude of circumstances and catastrophic emotions that followed the closing that vision will never occur.

As, I reflect back while writing this, I'm shocked that I could even have desire to go through those motions again. I think at the time, it was me just being fearing the uncertainty of what my next steps would be. Because, even thinking of another store afterwards was complete insanity. I will always enjoy the memories of what I had created and accomplished, but those desires are complete and over. Karma complete!

With the multitudes of circumstances that occurred that year, a very good friend of mine Mary Hoyer, referred to it as, **"my trial by fire"**.

Mary...I like to call her my Lighthouse because in extremely rough seas she always had the ability to guide me in. This so called "trial by fire" allowed me to grow and evolve more than

I ever thought possible.

Only the woman who has faced enormous loss may proclaim herself first among the immortals, because she is invulnerable to the wounds inflicted by mere humans.

Harriet Rubin, *The Art of Women, Age, and Power*

Even though some tried to cast shame, I always remembered that shame is when a person feels they're not good enough or is bad. Versus, someone that in a brief moment chose to do or say something stupid. There is a major difference between the two. **Anyone that tries to shame another... is someone that will always feel that they will never be enough themselves.**

It's for you to understand and embrace that we will all have moments of embarrassment or guilt, but to never allow another person's intentions to change your core beliefs.

The major difficulties that arose that year was like a domino effect. All starting with the moment I chose to close my store. Of course, I was questioning my original choice. To see so much devastation from that moment of clear conscious awareness. But, I was **DONE** with the financial roller coaster, and with the constant **NEED** to be "in" the store. I needed my freedom. And with that said, that store and what it represented at the time, was the farthest thing from freedom.

It was all so surreal, but so welcomed at the same time. Little did I know that you just don't really see all of the gifts until the dust really settles. I know now that everything played out exactly as it should have. It's just so hard to understand that while you're in the moment.

I was not a victim of any circumstance. In fact in life I choose to never to be a victim or a villain, but to be truly a **student in life.**

The ensemble of relationships that both helped me and supported me I am forever thankful for. Some were trying to support me, while others felt that their support should have been accepted without disobedience. To say that I felt betrayed and hurt is an understatement.

I fully realize that we will all take away our own stories and experiences from those very pivotal moments in time. This is just my way of saying, that I have chosen forgiveness...and that I have moved on. To those who were involved, they can have their story and they will find comfort there. But this is mine!

It was a very cold Chicago winter night in November of 2012, as I was reassembling my life. I was living with someone temporarily. I had just arrived back at this one particular friend's home, after working all day. When this person asked me to please come into the living room because she wanted to talk about something.

As I sat there listening to how upset she was, and how she wanted me to see the situation *her way*, I could immediately sympathize with how frustrating the whole dilemma was. But, it was how she conveyed her perspective, I felt that it was not only belittling, but her need to defame my character on top of it...was more than I could handle. At one point I knew that we just needed to separate. Especially me, from this very traumatic experience. So, I decided to leave that conversation, and her house immediately.

As the heated "discussion" continued, I decided not engage in too much dialog. Why infuriate an already intense situation. Plus, I was on sensory overload. I was completely mentally and emotionally exhausted after everything that I had gone through that year. I just wanted…and needed to leave.

So I got up, apologized for any difficult misunderstandings or should I say I tried to talk…unfortunately I was doing the ugly cry. Some may know how that goes, when you can't even really assemble your words. Because I was a blubbering mess, and girl when I say that I was a hot mess…I was! I was so emotionally raw. There was nothing left of my strength to hold it together anymore.

The anger was all around me…like a mist and it was literally suffocating me. I needed to walk away from that huge mess of a conversation. It's when I got about 15 to 20 feet away from that heated mess of a conversation, that I felt it.

It was though I had walked into some type of sunshine pouring through a window on a beautiful day (when in reality it was a cold, dark winter night). The noise and confusion of why this was all happening suddenly went mute. Such a wonderful feeling of peace came over me. It was so clear, my realization in that moment. While the sounds of yelling were still rang in my ears, I was totally **not** connected to the names that I was being called.

I didn't even realize what I was experiencing in that moment. It actually took me several days to process the whole situation. As I sit here and type out what I was experiencing, it was as though someone had put an invisible barrier (shield) around me and everything that was being thrown at me was just bouncing off this invisible wall. That was it...my graduation day! I became a full card carrying member of the **SELF-ACCEPTANCE CLUB** that night, through my own empowerment.

Yep, all those years of so called self-improvement books, classes and personal awareness moments didn't mean diddle. It was that night when I **CHOSE** not to believe the accusations that were being hurled upon me. **That was the day I woke up and chose not to absorb or affiliate with that OPINION...OR ANYONE ELSES GOING FORWORD.**

I felt total awareness, comfort, and knowing that this shame that was being placed on me-was NOT who I was, but a projection of their own. I felt **WHOLE**, total and complete. I shut out the chaos and was so connected to this source. Reminding me of my importance and self-value. It was as they say...priceless. I literally felt bathed in comfort and EASE! But that didn't mean, that I didn't have some healing to do...because boy did I...and lots of it!

Chapter Seventeen

...stand for something or fall for anything!

Some seek fame, others wealth, some both, I feel that **certainty/knowing/clarity** should be valued much more than fame and wealth. Having a firm conviction, a knowing without question, is beyond any outside accolade that can be offered to you. **That total clarity is the engine that will drive a whole person.**

People mistakenly confuse a desire to be whole, with perfectionism. Perfectionism as I have already discussed in a previous chapter of this book is a complete falsehood.

Strive to be a whole person, complete on your own, then that desire for perfectionism may fall away or at least quiet down. You become whole by discovering your boundaries. While not being afraid of shining a light on your strengths, as well as your weaknesses. Finding comfort with the balance.

I always knew of my laser sharp focus, intention, and most important of all my, total clarity of choice (though it was challenged at times). My whole life, I always felt that this was something that everyone possessed, and was comfortable in. That ability to have the confidence/courage to make their own choices. This seems to be such a simple sentence. But I know now, how much of a gift that really. What is that phrase again...*stand for something or fall for anything*. I have my own connection to this phrase now, you must believe in yourself and the truths for which you stand. Even though others may not agree. Because if you dare to stand for your own truths, others might find that threatening, and some may even feel that consequences should occur with that stance.

I would think the need for happiness, pleasure, and comfort would be a basic direction for everyone's life. Along with the fact of wishing that for other people. Sadly not everybody wishes us well. But I have now discovered how exciting our lives can be when we're free of negative influences. Carry yourself proud and be a commanding presence of perseverance.

...discovering my true elegance!

A commanding presence is walking through life with EASE. Not that negative things won't happen, because believe me they still do. This type of awareness, it will help you navigate through the negative events a lot easier. Because when you realize that there is nothing being done purposely to malign you, only to teach you, then the beauty of EASE will engulf you.

People may try to malign you, not support you. Perhaps never quite understand or even like you. But that's okay. That just means you're in the wrong place. EASE, through empowerment, is my life's work now. Knowing, no matter what happens to you in life, having the courage to walk through life with EASE-can bring such joy!

One must be aware that being repressed and living in fear of expressing your own individual desire's in life, is a prison. Pretending, can be even more corrosive to your soul. Pretending on so many levels, pretending to be happy, pretending to be kind to others. I have personally experienced people **pretending.** Pretending to support me, then using those vulnerable moments to talk about me negatively.

Finding the courage to be vulnerable while seeking personal self-acceptance and authenticity is the only way you will find peace in life. We all have our own unique way of handling things in life. We all carry ourselves in different fashions and rhythms. One is not more superior than the other. True successes in life is not being a victim of your circumstances, but seeing the beauty of your choices.

During this time of healing…I never felt more whole. This vulnerability stripped away the last of my barriers. Those layers of life that we use to protect ourselves. This brought such an awareness, a clarity of my own elegance-of being.

This 'trial by fire' inspired me to write these last pages and I want to end it with my own perception of how we all can implement this *feeling* of **being enough. Of** feeling whole in our lives. As I have already said, I desire to find EASE in my life! Even just saying the word EASE. The mere sound of the word, as I pronounce it, brings me such calm.

I feel so strongly about finding the importance of this word and applying it. It's now apart of my life's work. So much so that I actually created 8 steps to help remind me how to strengthen it. This is my version of what so many teachers have been talking about for many, many years. Mine, of course, has it's own unique twist on it, I feel that it encapsulates everything in a very simple and practical formula.

The 8 Secrets to "Get Your EASE On!"

EASE
- **Enough**
- **Allowing**
- **Surrender**
- **EMPOWERMENT**

1. Be Yourself…Be Unique!

Because like Oscar Wilde said, "everybody else is taken."

It takes a long time to grow-up.

Maturity is an emotion…not an age!

Are you living your best Life?

Create a side hustle. With time you will discover your true passion and what makes you unique from all others.

You are ENOUGH! Remember self-acceptance NOT self-improvement.

Becomes EMPOWERMENT!

Find your own style, Beige is basic. Don't dress like everyone else!

Find your best self-expression through style.

2. Be a Healing Presence!

Be the light of LOVE so strong…that nothing or no one can penetrate it with negativity.
Let others be the King and Queen, for just a moment.
It takes more elegance to step OUT of the lime light and let others shine.
People never forget those that make them feel good.
Don't forget that your home is a healing place and sanctuary.
No matter the size or the location.
The first and most important soul mate is yourself!

3. Be Self Motivated!

This might be hard for some and not others, but always find motivation and strength to make your own choices. Never find motivation at the expense of another. Otherwise you're motivated by ego…and that is not ELEGANT.

4. Be Open!

To RECEIVE! Open or shift your perception.
ALLOW!
Change your perspective!
Nothing is gained from being rigid.
Live and LOVE excuse free.

5. **Be Mysterious!**

Obtain elegant detachment!
Lean back and relax.
Learn when to use feminine and masculine energies.
Embrace your femininity by being emotionally balanced.
Remember Mona Lisa's smile? People to this day are still trying to figure what she was thinking about. She created so much mystery with just a smile.
Strong inner confidence is obtained through the elegance of aging, that is called maturity.

6. **Surrender!**

Allow life to unfold naturally.
Many will say that they do…surrender. But to really totally surrender can very difficult.
But you need to at least TRY!

7. **Be a Time Traveler!**

Be all ages…but now do it with the elegance and maturity. It's not by changing your style of dress to appear more youthful. It just means to let go and relax into life as you were back when you were a child, before heavy responsibilities set in.
Don't act like a child (temper tantrums)…but have a

child-like wonderment in life. Don't be afraid of being silly and quirky.

People like to be around those who enjoy life!

Be the creative director of the life you want!

Ask questions. Don't demand answers.

Then allow the universe to align with those answers in time.

8. Be Commanding...NOT Demanding!

Be positive and inspire...supporting people draws them into your space. Ask others about their life...be engaging.

Being ELEGANT has nothing to do with being the center of attention or by being the loudest, the joke-teller, or the one that can always "*do it better.*"

Nor is it about ROCKING the latest labels!

Last but not least, aim to be whole...NOT perfect!

We would all LOVE to appear beautiful to everyone but that's not possible. **Strive to be comfortable with your own beauty.** And remember that you will always be beautiful in your families eye's and those who you have chosen to LOVE!

As strongly as I believe in these elements of EASE and how important it is to incorporate them into our lifestyle. There is also what I like to call the nasty ninja's. The aspects that try to prevent us from truly applying EASE in our lives. They're the following:

- Toxic Bosses/People
- Jealous Friends and Family Members.
- Being Obsessed-stuck in the concept of perfectionism (your way is the only way).
- Troubled Self-Confidence/Undeserving
- The Disease to Please.
- The To-Do-List/No Time/Excuses.
- Being Youth Obsessed (plastic surgeries).
- Burden to be Constantly Fashionable.
- Difficult Husbands/Family Issues.
- Myopic Perspectives.
- Justification
- Arrogance

Always, find the strength to prevail. Just pick up this book/journal and reread certain chapters to remind yourself of your true purpose of discovering the importance of finding **EASE in your life** and of course **learn to SURRENDER** *to LOVE.*

Your greatest battle is to become an authentic spirit...especially in the face of adversity.

Note To Self

Note To Self

Note To Self

EPILOGUE

Just for play...because we all need to remember how to!

Have you ever noticed that in the back of some magazines there may be a page where editors would interview someone asking what their likes and dislikes are? I LOVE those pages, and that's how I'm going to close out this book/journal. For several reasons...life is about finding out what you like and don't like.

Philosophies and fabulousities that I can't live without!

1. Everybody likes to be recognized...take time to smile or say **Hi** to a stranger. You just might just make his or her day.
2. LOVE ATTRACTS LOVE
3. Chocolate and White Wine!
4. Esoteric Arts and Mind/Body Connection...it fascinates me!

5. Painting!

6. My dog Henri! Be kind to animals!

7. My greatest past time indulgences are manicures, pedicures, massages, binge watching 1940's Film Noir, and writing.

8. Long slow kisses that last all night!

9. Traveling for pleasure...possibly discovering cool Artist's Retreats!

10. Cooking-keep it simple...LOVE the textures and colors of a beautiful plate of **healthy** food!

11. LOVE Fashion...hate malls!

12. Flowers.

13. Creating a COLLECTIVE and SELECTIVE place to live.

14. The magic begins at I AM...because you're the Creative Director of your life! Find your own inner strength and trust your own inner voice!

15. Having that inner RADIANCE, and develop the subtleties of allure.

16. I accept your limited perception of ME!

17. LOVE going out to dinner and/or drinks with friends.

18. Shoes...not expensive but definitely a touch sexy!

19. My BED…yes you read that right…I LOVE my BED! Not just for the obvious, sleeping and you know but for just being there when I want to curl up and read! Finding it never to fussy…so that I would be afraid to mess the covers.

20. Holistic skin care, prefer only pure organic ingredients for skin care!

21. Find your own signature scent or perfume. Find one maybe two…and make it a personal trademark.

22. LOVE dresses in the summer.

23. Red Lipstick-Everyone needs to find that right shade of red for herself.

24. Never take yourself to "seriously"…and never think that your opinion is the only right answer. If you're feeling negative, mean, and ornery…stay home!

25. Go find yourself…because everyone else is taken, as Oscar Wilde has stated.

Note To Self

FROM THE AUTHOR:

I hoped that you have enjoyed this book/journal that I have written. Though I'm not a career writer, I enjoy creating things to inspire others, and this is just another form.

Many years ago I needed something like this book/journal. Now I have fulfilled that desire so that maybe someone else can find hope and possibly find the answers to something that is as elusive, and as important as (self) LOVE.

> *We're consumed about how to do it right, how to make it successful. Over come the problems and survive its failures. As we know it's not that simple. We talk of it lightly not realizing how powerful and long lasting it can be. Some are even tortured by LOVE not properly expressed. LOVE seems to be that essence that we all need to fill up our gaping wounds from the past, but it also provides us with a grace to guide us through the future. Simply put, LOVE feeds our soul!*
>
> **Thomas Moore**

LOVE ATTRACTS LOVE...
thank you for taking the time,
Gail J. Kueker
Never Got The Memo.info
Send me your questions and comments to:
INSPIREMEETOO@gmail.com
Would LOVE to hear from you!

www.ingramcontent.com/pod-product-compliance
Lightning Source LLC
Chambersburg PA
CBHW071908290426
44110CB00013B/1321